Lavish Legacies

*Baltimore Album and Related Quilts
in the Collection of the
Maryland Historical Society*

by Jennifer Faulds Goldsborough

with Barbara K. Weeks
photography by Jeff D. Goldman

Funded by a generous grant from the
T. Rowe Price Associates Foundation Publications Fund

Maryland Historical Society
Baltimore, Maryland

Publication of this catalogue of a segment of the textile collection of the Maryland Historical Society has been made possible by the T. Rowe Price Associates Foundation Publication Fund.

Copyright: 1994 by the Maryland Historical Society, Baltimore

Designed, typeset, and printed by S & S Graphics, Laurel, MD

Figure 1 Detail of Catalogue 32.

"Give her of the fruits of her hands
and let her works praise her in the gates."

Proverbs, 31:31

Contents

Acknowledgments	xi
Lavish Legacies: Baltimore Album Quilts	1
What Is A Baltimore Album Quilt?	3
How Did Baltimore Album Quilts Develop?	7
Who Made Baltimore Album Quilts?	13
Why Were Baltimore Album Quilts Made?	25
Where Did The Designs On Baltimore Album Quilts Come From And What Do They Mean?	27
What Techniques Were Used On Baltimore Album Quilts?	34
What Do Baltimore Album Quilts Tell Us About The Women Who Made Them?	35
Domestic Spheres And Home Circles: The Dimensions Of Early Nineteenth-century Baltimore Women's Lives	37
Catalogue Of The Baltimore Album And Related Quilts In The Maryland Historical Society Collection	47
Selected Bibliography	121

x

Acknowledgements

The Maryland Historical Society has an exceptional and extensive textile collection including more than two hundred fine quilts. Because these fragile legacies from the past cannot frequently be handled or exhibited, they have been little known to the public, women's historians, or quilt scholars and enthusiasts. More than six years ago, the Maryland Historical Society initiated a series of quilt exhibitions to bring well-deserved attention to the collection and to encourage the study of these quilts and the women who made them.

It was our hope that during the course of the exhibition series, money would be found to publish the results of our research and to provide illustrations of the quilts. Such a publication serves several purposes: to record and disseminate the latest information, to encourage on-going study, to make the collection more widely known to an audience who may not be able to visit Baltimore, and to provide an in-depth resource of designs and history for scholars so that the quilts themselves will not have to be handled as much in the future. We are especially grateful to the T. Rowe Price Associates Foundation for its sensitive understanding of this mission which has resulted in the establishment of a revolving publication fund to publish this *Lavish Legacies* collection catalogue and additional books as time goes on. It is comforting to know that the local business community is dedicated to working with the Maryland Historical Society to assure the preservation and study of the past for the enrichment of the future.

The first exhibition in the Maryland Historical Society series, *Maryland Quilts and Their Crazy Offspring*, took place in the fall of 1988 and featured late-nineteenth-century crazy quilts from the collection. The second exhibition, *Lavish Legacies: Baltimore Album Quilts 1845-1855* is the occasion of this publication of the Maryland Historical Society collection of Baltimore album and related quilts made during the mid-nineteenth century at the time the Maryland Historical Society itself was founded.

The *Lavish Legacies* project has involved the conservation of a number of antique quilts, several years of in-depth research by a diverse group of scholars, the display of thirty quilts during a two-part exhibition along with other related artifacts, and the compilation of this volume. The exhibition was made possible, in part, by a generous grant from The National Endowment for the Arts, a federal agency. Additional exhibition funding was provided by Warm Products C & T Publishing, That Patchwork Place, J. Dashew Inc., P&B Textiles, WJZ-TV, F. W. Haxel Co., Inc.

Any project of this scale requires the help and support of many, many people. We wish to acknowledge the extraordinary efforts of the following here:

Virginia Pledger whose superb conservation work made it possible to display a number of these fragile textiles and whose experience helped us understand how they were made. Funding for conservation was provided, in part, by a special grant from The National Endowment for the Arts, a federal agency, matched by funds from the local quilt guilds listed below.

It was Karen Ringrose, an experienced quilt curatorial volunteer whose knowledge, enthusiasm, energy, and good-will made the whole project move from dream to reality.

Present and past members of the Gallery staff, especially Gregory Weidman, Barbara Weeks, Rosemary Gately, Catherine Rogers, Susan Kleckner, Mary Beth Paszkiewicz, Karen Matter, Katherine Marston, and Erin Gamse expended the thousands of hours of curatorial work and professional research which are reflected here.

A number of fine college interns also contributed excellent work to this study: Jennifer Greene, Katherine Behrens, Aimee C. Einstein.

Present and past members of the Registrars Office including Elizabeth Gordon, Elizabeth Heydt, Katherine Carey, and Merrill Lavine have helped handle, store, record, and display the quilts in this study.

We are grateful for the superb photographs by Jeff D. Goldman. And Michael Shea of the Business Office, Penny Catzen, Head Librarian, and Jennifer Bryan, Curator of Manuscripts, provided frequent and willing help.

Hugh Andrew of the Maryland Historical Society and contractors Mark Ward, Werner Hauger, and Bob Rogers with their teams provided much-needed assistance with the exhibition installation.

Staff, interns, and volunteer docents from the Education Department led by Judy Van Dyke have ensured that the information about the quilts made sense and was of interest to our visitors. In addition, their out-reach quilt projects have brought new audiences to our celebratory exhibition of Baltimore album quilts.

We are, of course, especially grateful to the generous donors of these quilts who have conscientiously sought to preserve the unique heritage of Maryland over the past hundred and fifty years by contributing to the collection of the Maryland Historical Society. And we also thank the private collectors whose objects were cheerfully lent to enhance the exhibition and to provide exemplary illustrations for this book.

During the course of this study, we have discovered that the quilt world is a very special one in which the generosity and sharing of information and experience by scholars and specialists is nonpareil. Among those quilt specialists and women's studies authorities from across the country who have been particularly helpful are Barbara Brackman, Elly Sienkiewicz, Gloria Allen, Joyce Gross, Anita Schackelford, Louise Townsend, Julie Roy Jeffrey, Elaine Hedges, Helen Jean Burn, Nancy Tuckhorn of the DAR Museum, Anita Jones of The Baltimore Museum of Art, Barbara Luck of the Abby Aldrich Rockefeller Folk Art Center in Williamsburg, and the Rev. Edwin Schell of the Baltimore Washington United Methodist Historical Society at Lovely Lane Church. John McGrain was particularly helpful in providing relevant local history. Numerous museum and historic house curators have shared their collections and knowledge with our scholars, and we have also relied heavily on the exceptional quilt histories and various state quilt documentation studies published during recent decades. Certainly, without the efforts of previous Baltimore album quilt historians Dr. William Rush Dunton, Jr. and Dena Katzenberg, we would have been unable to go forward with the study of these magnificent examples of textile art. We are greatly indebted to Gloria Allen, Joyce Gross, and Louise Townsend for their gracious and sensitive content and copy editing for this publication; any errors are the responsibility of the authors. Erin Gamse diligently helped shepherd the manuscript through publication.

We have been the beneficiaries of enormous encouragement from the staffs and members of the American Quilt Study Group, The National Quilting Association, the American Quilter's Society, the writers and editors of numerous quilters' magazines, and a number of quilt guilds. We have been especially fortunate in receiving expert volunteer help and substantial funding for the project from the Annapolis Quilt Guild, the Baltimore Heritage Quilt Guild, and the Eternal Quilters, Inc. guild.

In fact, the project created so much excitement and enthusiasm among contemporary quilters that a special quilt guild was established by Janice Carlson, Toni Carr, Mimi Dietrich, and Jeana Kimball in the spring of 1993 expressly to support the quilt projects of the Maryland Historical Society. Within just one year, the national membership of this Baltimore Appliqué Society numbered almost two-hundred exceedingly active individuals. These enthusiasts have been without peer; they have successfully raised many thousands of dollars for the conservation, study, and exhibition of the Maryland Historical Society quilts through a variety of activities; in addition, they have provided thousands of hours of expert volunteer work in preparing the quilts for exhibition, planning and providing educational activities, and by developing numerous programming opportunities, etc. Their devotion and confidence have generated the energy that has driven the project; and they have been the best publicity authorities and public relations staff anyone could wish for—their taps into the "quilters' grape-vine" have brought visitors from as far away as England, Holland, France, Japan, and Australia, as well as letters and photographs from numerous private collectors and owners of antique Baltimore album quilts. *Lavish Legacies* truly became a perfect blend of community support and cooperation combined with museum staff work, and like a quilt made of many snippets of fabric, the result has been far greater than the sum of its parts.

Dennis A. Fiori
Executive Director

Jennifer F. Goldsborough
Chief Curator

Lavish Legacies: Baltimore Album Quilts

*Every experience deeply felt in life needs
to be passed along—whether it be through words
and music, chiseled in stone, painted with a brush,
or sewn with a needle, it is a way of reaching for immortality.*

Thomas Jefferson

by Jennifer Faulds Goldsborough

Nineteenth-century American quilts are known the world over for their inventiveness and beauty; most highly regarded of all are the exquisite album quilts made in the Baltimore, Maryland vicinity between about 1845 and 1855. Baltimore album quilts were first identified by William Rush Dunton, Jr., M.D. As the developer, early in the twentieth century, of occupational therapy for the mentally ill, Dr. Dunton promoted quilting for his "nervous ladies" at the famed Sheppard-Pratt Hospital. His search within the Baltimore area for old quilts to use as models uncovered about a dozen, similar, mid-nineteenth-century local quilts which exemplified extraordinary beauty and skill. They inspired Dunton to undertake a serious study of quilts and to become a quilter himself. His privately published 1946 volume, *Old Quilts*, illustrated the premier examples which he called Baltimore album quilts.

The genre was codified and brought to international attention by the major exhibition and accompanying catalogue entitled *Baltimore Album Quilts* by Dena S. Katzenberg, Consultant Curator to The Baltimore Museum of Art. Between 1980 and 1982, that exhibition travelled to the Museum of Fine Arts, Houston, and the Metropolitan Museum of Art, New York, before returning to The Baltimore Museum of Art. Since that exhibition, dealer and auction prices for the finest, original Baltimore album quilts have soared to equal those for "old master" paintings. And tens of thousands of women around the world have experienced the joy of creating new quilts in the Baltimore album quilt tradition. They have been inspired and guided by classes, lectures, and books by talented quilting teachers such as Mimi Dietrich, Jeana Kimball, Anita Shackelford, Elly Sienkiewicz, and many others who have combined knowledge of heritage with clear directions for making quilts in the Baltimore album manner.

The Maryland Historical Society houses the largest and most representative collection of authentic Baltimore album quilts. The collection includes more than two dozen prime examples as well as a number of appliquéd chintz and red-and-green appliquéd quilts, which were the precursors of the Baltimore album quilt style. Scholars have now assembled files of information on more than 300 surviving examples of this very specific textile art; study of this greatly expanded number of known Baltimore album quilts has enhanced and enriched the information gleaned from examining the quilts in the Maryland Historical Society collection.

Figure 2 Detail of cut-paper type square from Baltimore album quilt, 1845-1846 (see Catalogue 23 for entire quilt).

Figure 3 Detail of typical red-and-green appliquéd square used on a Baltimore album quilt, c. 1848 (see Catalogue 28 for entire quilt).

Figure 4 Detail of elaborate, pictorial, layered appliqué on Baltimore album quilt, 1845-1848 (see Catalogue 23 for entire quilt).

Figure 5 Detail of padded and embroidered square from Baltimore album quilt, c. 1849 (see Catalogue 15 for entire quilt).

What Is A Baltimore Album Quilt?

The phrase Baltimore album quilt is a modern term referring to a specific type of nineteenth-century bedcovering with distinct characteristics. Baltimore album quilts were composed of individual cloth squares of uniform size arranged in a grid pattern. Occasionally squares of double- or quadruple-size were grouped toward the center of the quilt to provide a focus reminiscent of earlier medallion-style quilts. In a few instances, the squares were arranged "on point" in diagonal rows. With few exceptions, Baltimore album quilt squares were large, usually approximately sixteen inches square. The quilts, too, were usually square and of quite large size. Curiously, there was little organizational consistency and squares might be oriented in many directions—sometimes radiating from the center, sometimes all facing one direction, sometimes in a seemingly random arrangement in which one or two squares appeared to be upside-down (see Catalogue 11).

Baltimore album quilt squares were enhanced with a variety of intricate appliqué designs of two sorts. One type of design was created by folding and cutting complex, symmetrical, snowflake-like paper patterns (Figure 2). This sort of appliqué was related to German *scherenschnitte*, the art of making delicate and lacy cut-paper designs; this style of appliqué was favored among the German-American residents of southern Pennsylvania and northern Maryland. Simplified versions of this type of appliqué designs such as reel-and-leaf, crossed laurel leaves, and fleur-de-lis patterns were very popular on the red-and-green appliqué quilts of the mid-nineteenth century and became part of the common American quilt design vocabulary (Figure 3). These designs continued to appear on Baltimore album quilts, especially in corner positions on the quilts, throughout the 1840s and 1850s. The most delicate cut-paper designs, resembling lace or cob webs, usually appear on Baltimore album quilt squares made before 1850.

The second type of appliqué work on Baltimore album quilts featured realistic, pictorial designs of *compotiers* of fruit, local landmarks, ships, people, symbols of organizations, and especially vases, wreaths, and baskets of flowers. These naturalistic designs were created by the clever manipulation and layering of imported and domestic fabrics (Figure 4). Details were embroidered or inked, and a sense of three dimensionality was often created with padding or fabric selection and placement (Figure 5).

The transitional stage of development of the very earliest, pre-1848, Baltimore album quilts was sometimes revealed by the inclusion of chintz appliquéd or finely pieced squares. Both chintz and pieced star or hexagonal/octagonal pieced designs appeared too infrequently for them to be considered significant alternatives to the cut-paper and realistic pictorial appliqué designs in defining the Baltimore album style.

Many Baltimore album quilts were assembled without sashing. Some of the earliest had red sawtooth sashing strips, which resembled pieced work but often were appliquéd (see Catalogue 13, 14, 15). Plain fabric strips or repetitive printed designs cut from striped fabric were sometimes used as sashing (see Catalogue 12, 18, 24, 26).

Border designs also varied widely on Baltimore album quilts, ranging from no borders at all to simple bands of plain-colored cloth, calico, or imported chintz. Appliquéd borders might be restrained geometric patterns, or decoratively swagged drapery designs, or sumptuously elegant and elaborate floral vines (Figures 6, 7, 8).

Baltimore album quilts were masterpieces of needlework and often exemplified numerous skills. The visual impact relied on the selection and variety of costly fabrics, the intricacy and detail of the appliquéd designs, and the special effects of padding, fabric manipulation, embroidery, and inking. The quilting itself often was of secondary importance to the designs, fabrics, appliqués, and embroidery. Only occasionally did quilters indulge in fancy feather, scroll, or other pictorial patterns for their fine, careful quilting stitches. Most Baltimore album quilts were quilted in simple diamond, square, or other linear patterns. Many Baltimore album quilts were never quilted at all; some appliquéd tops seem to have been deliberately finished off with a light backing or lining as bedspreads. Others survived in an unfinished state. A considerable number of appliquéd but unassembled quilt squares in the Baltimore album style also survive.

Quilts of this sort were called albums after the popularity of album books during the early-nineteenth century. Young women treasured watercolor sketches, sentimental verses, dried flowers, the autographs of friends and other mementos in pretty books called albums (Figure 9). Album quilts were like a collection of different cloth pages laid side by side instead of bound between covers. In addition, many album quilt squares were inscribed with verses, names, and dates, which made them sentimental reminders, like album books, of an individual's friends and family.

Album quilts of diverse appliquéd squares were also made in other mid-Atlantic regions such as Pennsylvania, Delaware, New Jersey and New York, but those usually were simpler in design and employed a smaller square size than their Baltimore cousins. The dates and names written on quilts meeting the Baltimore album quilt description help us determine that, indeed, these magnificent textiles originated in Baltimore City or the immediately surrounding area and flourished around 1850. The earliest dated square in this genre, which was examined by the Maryland Historical Society staff, is inscribed with the year 1842 (Figure 10). The dates on the most elaborate quilts and Maryland Institute Fair records indicate that the style was diminishing in popularity by 1854, although Maryland quilts continued to be influenced by this style until the Civil War period.

Figure 6 Detail of early, red, appliquéd sawtooth border on Baltimore album quilt, c. 1845-1850 (see Catalogue 13 for entire quilt).

Figure 7 Detail of appliquéd swag border on Baltimore album quilt (see Catalogue 10 for entire quilt).

Figure 8 Detail of floral vine border on Baltimore album quilt (see catalogue 16 for entire quilt).

Figure 9 Watercolor-painted flowers from a page in a young Maryland woman's album book, 1845. From the Prints and Photographs Division, Maryland Historical Society.

Figure 10 Detail of square dated 1842 from a Baltimore album quilt, Maryland Historical Society.

How Did Baltimore Album Quilts Develop?

What factors led to the emergence of this magnificent type of quilt in Baltimore at such a specific period of time? First, one must consider Baltimore itself. During the early decades of the nineteenth century, Baltimore experienced a surge of growth and prosperity far greater than that of any other city in North America. Not only did it become, for a time, the second largest city and port in the country, but one of the most sophisticated and fashion-conscious centers in America as well. Visitors commented regularly that Baltimore women were the most beautiful and best-dressed in the nation during the early decades of the century.[1] A distinct local taste for elaboration and great richness in household furnishings developed, which manifested itself in the ornate, repoussé-encrusted silver created by Samuel Kirk and Andrew Ellicott Warner and in the painted and gilded furniture made in the shops of the Finlay brothers and others (Figures 11, 12).

Enormous quantities of English and French fabrics poured into the port of Baltimore. Maryland's own textile mills were burgeoning. Fabrics in vast variety at reasonable cost were more available to local Baltimore women than to women anywhere else in the United States at this moment. These readily available textiles were combined with the local taste for over-blown ornamentation to create quilts that were celebrations of abundance.

No artistic or craft style emerges in a vacuum. The progenitors of Baltimore album quilts may be found in the chintz appliquéd quilts which were popular as fancy bedcovers, especially among the Southern gentry, during the first half of the nineteenth century and in the red-and-green geometric appliqué style, which became particularly popular among mid-Atlantic German-Americans during the 1840s (see Catalogue 1-6).

In 1850, the population of Baltimore was almost evenly divided between those of British background and those of German heritage, many with strong ties to southern Pennsylvania. As these two groups interacted in neighborhoods, businesses, churches, and benevolent organizations, their quilting traditions blended into a new and unique style. It has been popular in recent years to substitute the image of a quilt for the older melting-pot simile to symbolize the ethnic diversity and blending of the United States. The flamboyant album quilts of Baltimore in the 1850s are perfect illustrations of the appropriateness of this symbolic convention!

Quilted bedcovers came to America in the seventeenth and eighteenth centuries as whole-cloth quilts, often of great luxury. In fact, bed furnishings of all sorts represented the ultimate in extravagant household goods among British colonists. Bedding comprised the most valuable possessions in house inventories and the most desirable items in a bride's trousseau. In this sense, the impetus to provide and possess gorgeous bedcovers such as Baltimore album quilts was a natural descendant of the royal, medieval and Renaissance custom of outfitting and maintaining costly beds of state, which were rarely if ever slept in. Many whole-cloth quilts were made of imported Indian *palampores* or imitations of such textiles with a central Tree-of-Life motif. From these developed the notion of central medallion quilts, often made by cutting up expensive, imported chintz and rearranging the pieces to create new designs. This method provided a means by which a small amount of exorbitantly costly cloth could be used to provide pattern over a much larger surface.

Only those American women who could afford grandly decorated houses, leisure time to pursue the production of luxury goods, and the price of fabrics sometimes costing the equivalent of $100 or more per yard could indulge in making chintz medallion quilts. Women of elite English background had sometimes been trained in the *broderie perse* technique by which fabric designs were heavily embroidered, then cut-out and applied to plain fabric with further embroidery (Figure 13).[2] Some Maryland chintz-appliquéd quilts were stitched with feather or other embroidery stitches in the *broderie perse* manner, others were blind-stitched

Figure 11 Silver teapot in the heavily ornamented Baltimore repoussé style by Samuel Kirk and Son, Baltimore, c. 1845. Although few Baltimore album quiltmakers could have afforded such an object, they might well have been familiar with such silver from shop windows; both repoussé silver and Baltimore album quilts exemplify the local taste for floral elaboration in house furnishings. Gift of Mr. and Mrs. John J. Neubauer, Jr., 87.133.56

Figure 12 Detail of painted and gilded ottoman made in Baltimore, c. 1825, attributed to Hugh Finlay. Gift of Edward P. Crummer, 59.13.8

Figure 13 Detail of *broderie perse* chintz-appliquéd square on Baltimore album quilt, c. 1846-1847 (see Catalogue 25 for entire quilt).

to give the effect that the chintz pieces were part of the background fabric. The gorgeous chintzes from England, France, and even early American printing houses resulted in rich, vivid, highly naturalistic floral and fruit designs, which often were repeated in the chintz strip borders. As the nineteenth century progressed, the medallion style with its center square or rectangle surrounded by a series of concentric borders led quilt makers to become increasingly familiar with making a quilt of segments rather than from a whole piece or seamed pieces of the same cloth. By the 1830s, some chintz-appliqué quilts were made of uniformly sized squares organized according to the grid or diagonal "on point" scheme, which became part of the Baltimore album quilt style (see Catalogue 6).

Also around 1840, another type of appliqué quilt emerged in the mid-Atlantic region. This style has been called red-and-green because of the predominance, if not exclusive use, of that color scheme with a white or pale muslin background. This seems to have been a more middle-class kind of quilt than the chintz-appliquéd style. Strangely, quilt scholars have found little or no evidence of quiltmaking in Germany at this time; however, the geometric designs on many red-and-green quilts resemble those found on other German folk arts and crafts.[3] These appliquéd designs, although often derived from nature, are much less realistic than those found on chintz quilts (see Catalogue 1, 2).

The red-and-green color scheme probably derived from the new availability of fabrics, which heretofore had been too expensive and too rare for middle-class housewives to rely on for their quilt designs. The red was dyed with madder according to the very involved and time-consuming Turkey red process. Plain or small-figured green fabric still often required a multi-step dying process with blue and yellow colors dyed over each other to create green. True to the contrariness of human nature, red and green fabrics became fashionable for quilts in large part because they were costly and hard to dye.

The appliqué patterns for red-and-green quilts were made by folding and cutting paper to create symmetrical shapes. These quilts were made from squares of the same pattern laid side by side, usually within a red-and-green appliqué border (see Catalogue 2).

The earliest Baltimore album quilts combine some characteristic red-and-green cut-paper squares with

Figure 14 Detail of appliquéd chintz floral wreath on Maryland album quilt, c. 1840 (see Catalogue 6 for entire quilt).

Figure 15 Detail of layered appliqué floral wreath on Baltimore album quilt, 1852, perhaps inspired by printed chintzes such as Figure 14 (see Catalogue 7 for entire quilt).

some chintz-appliquéd squares and some floral squares in which plain and small-figured fabrics are cut out in shapes and manipulated to create naturalistic flowers. One 1846 quilt in the Maryland Historical Society collection has squares of each of these types (see Catalogue 25). In addition, the technical ancestry of this quilt is seen in the buttonhole and other fancy stitches used both on some of the chintz squares and used in the *broderie perse* manner on some of the calico appliquéd flowers.

Although chintz appliqué appeared less and less frequently as the Baltimore album quilt style developed and stuffed or layered plain and small-figured fabrics became more common, the red-and-green color scheme continued to predominate in Baltimore album quilts.

In comparing luxurious Maryland chintz-appliquéd quilts of the 1830s and 1840s with Baltimore album quilts with elaborately layered floral appliquéd squares and borders, it appears that the layered-appliqué technique was devised as a method to replicate the appearance of chintz by using less costly textiles. Today, the labor-intensive and practiced skill required to create these compositions is considered astonishing (Figures 14-19).

Figure 16 Detail of chintz appliquéd vase of flowers on Maryland album quilt, c. 1840 (see Catalogue 6 for entire quilt).

Figure 17 Detail of layered-appliqué vase of flowers on Baltimore album quilt, 1852 (see Catalogue 7 for entire quilt).

Figure 18 Detail of appliquéd and embroidered vase of flowers on Baltimore album quilt, c. 1850 (see Catalogue 30 for entire quilt).

Figure 19 Detail of appliquéd vase of flowers on Baltimore album quilt, c. 1850 (see Catalogue 26 for entire quilt).

11

Figure 20 Detail of elaborately inked inscription on Baltimore album quilt; the vast majority of the inked drawings and names on all fine Baltimore album quilts appear to have been executed by the same hand.

Figure 21 Detail of tiny cross-stitched initials on Baltimore album quilt; the use of cross-stitching for initials and names on Baltimore album quilts seems to be an early feature, which was dying out by 1846.

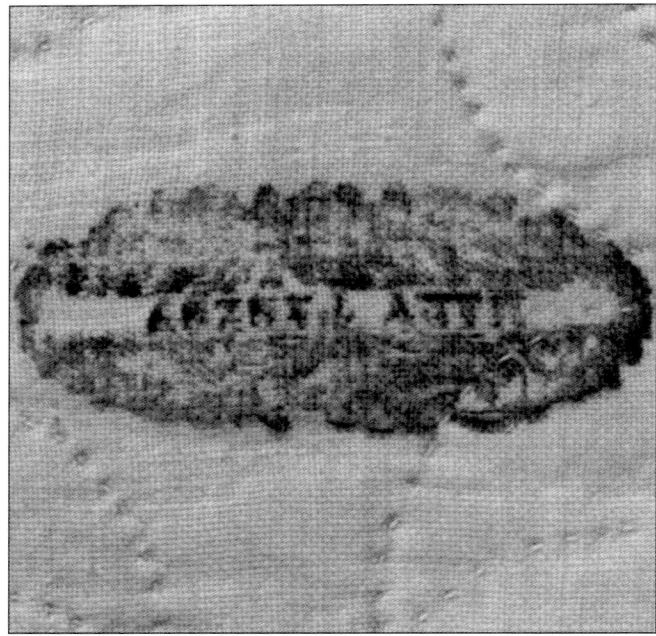

Figure 22 Detail of a stamped name on Baltimore album quilt; using small metal stamps for marking names on quilts was far more popular in Pennsylvania than in Maryland. When stamps appear on a Baltimore album quilt, the person named usually had recently moved from Pennsylvania or lived near that state's border.

Figure 23 Detail of individualistic, inked signature on a Baltimore album quilt; occasionally, the maker of a quilt square may have signed her name herself.

Who Made Baltimore Album Quilts?

Hundreds of names were inscribed on Baltimore album quilts. Most of these were exquisitely written in permanent ink by what appears to have been the same highly-skilled calligrapher. They were written in a very small, copper-plate script and were usually surrounded by diminutive, detailed cartouches or frames incorporating flowers, ribbons, birds, and other sentimental motifs (Figure 20). Since hundreds of names were inscribed in this manner, they may represent the recipient of a quilt, family or friends being memorialized, someone who contributed funds toward a quilt, as well as indicating an individual who may have been involved in making the square or quilt on which the name appeared. The later the date of the quilt, the more uniform and meticulous the handwriting seems to be.

Baltimore album quilt squares with very early dates (usually pre-1846) were sometimes marked with very small cross-stitched initials or names in the manner by which household linens were traditionally marked for identification (Figure 21). It is likely that these squares were stitched by the woman whose initials are embroidered on them.

Only rarely are stamped names found on Baltimore album quilts (Figure 22). Small pewter or other base-metal stamps were used for marking laundry and needlework and were particularly popular in Pennsylvania at this time. Those few that do appear on Maryland quilts seem to be on squares that originated close to the Pennsylvania border or are names with known Pennsylvania connections. In some instances, squares were marked with more individualistic inked names; most of these were probably actual signatures of someone associated with those squares (Figure 23).

Genealogical research into the names on Baltimore album quilts does not always tell us who made a particular quilt, but taken together, does provide information on the cultural and social groups associated with these textiles. It is very difficult to locate records about nineteenth-century women without knowing the names of their fathers and/or husbands. However, by pooling information from the 1850 census, city directories, church records, newspapers, other period records, and family histories, the identities of many dozens of women were determined.

This research confirms that these extraordinary quilts were primarily an urban product centering in Baltimore City and the immediate surrounding area. Of those found to have been made outside the city, most of those encountered were associated with Harford County to the north of Baltimore towards Pennsylvania. Visually, it appears that the farther from the city a quilt was made, the simpler it is in design and execution with very little layered appliqué; in other words, elaboration diminishes as distance from Baltimore increases.

In studying the entire body of surviving mid-nineteenth-century American album quilts, a small group may be distinguished from the Philadelphia area dating to the early 1840s. These are quite English in appearance and are characterized by many pink or rose-colored fabrics. The squares tend to be rather small and the designs more simple and geometric than the Baltimore quilts of the following two decades.

A larger group of album quilts survive that more closely resemble the archetypal Baltimore album quilts in their largely red-and-green color schemes, but they lack the most elaborate pictorial squares. Many of these evidently originated in southern Pennsylvania and northern Maryland in the region between the two metropolises. Without strong family histories, it is usually impossible to determine on which side of the state border a particular quilt was made. The population of this entire region was fairly fluid at the time, and much of the growth of Baltimore derived from the influx of Philadelphians and Pennsylvania-Germans. From the names and dates on album quilts, it seems that the concept may have originated under English influence in Philadelphia and then moved southward picking up the red-and-green emphasis and the *scherenschnitte* influence among the more rural German-American population. When it reached Baltimore, it exploded with the vitality of abundant fabrics and under the direction of a few particularly talented women into the very specific style that we recognize today. The rural version of album quilts continued to be made for several decades along the Pennsylvania-Maryland border.

Making Baltimore album quilts was a craze that lasted only about ten years, reaching its peak around 1850. The quilts were made by women whose economic status ranged across the broad spectrum of the middle-class: wives and daughters of farmers, butchers, mariners, tradesmen, preachers, craftsmen. The wealthiest women probably continued to make chintz quilts; the poorest women could afford neither cloth nor time to make quilts at all.

Baltimore album quilts were made by women who ranged in age from their late teens through their sixties and seventies. The largest age group were women in their twenties. Most people associated with Baltimore album quilts were members of Protestant churches, especially Methodist or German Reformed. This is consistent with the middle-class status of the makers; the established, old gentry of Maryland was primarily Episcopalian, while the newest and poorest German and Irish immigrants were Roman Catholic. The middle-class citizens of Baltimore were particularly sympathetic to the democratic, egalitarian, and temperance sentiments promoted by Methodist, German Reformed, Quaker, Baptist, and other Protestant preachers and tract writers.

Some Baltimore album quilts obviously were collections of designs and needlework by a number of different women whose names may be recorded on the quilts (see Catalogue 21, 23, 24, 25). But many Baltimore album quilts reveal the artistic efforts of just a few designers who may or may not also have stitched the quilts (see Catalogue 7, 8, 16, 18, 19). By studying more than 300 surviving Baltimore album quilts, distinctive characteristics of several major designers may be discerned, just as work by Monet, Renoir, and Degas may be distinguished in a group of French Impressionist paintings.

Dr. William R. Dunton, Dena Katzenberg, Elly Sienkiewicz, and others who have seriously studied Baltimore album quilts have been struck by the enormous similarity in design among many of the very finest Baltimore album quilt squares. It has been suggested that there was a professional quiltmaker who was responsible for the most distinctive and easily recognized work. The person most often proposed as this individual was a young woman named Mary Evans who was still a teenager living in the household of her widowed mother in 1850. This theory, largely promoted by antiques dealers and auction houses during the last decade, was sparked by Dr. Dunton's photographs and notes concerning seven unfinished Baltimore album quilt squares which were found in a trunk by descendants of Mary Evans (later Mrs. John Ford) (see Catalogue 32).[4] One of the squares, a large quadruple-size depiction of the Baltimore City Spring, was in the basted stage and the assumption was drawn, because it was unfinished, that it was Mary Evans's own work. The whereabouts of these seven squares was unknown for a number of decades.

As more and more surviving Baltimore album quilts were located and the seven Mary Evans squares were rediscovered and acquired by the Maryland Historical Society, the theory that Mary Evans had been the master quiltmaker of Baltimore became more and more suspect. The most cursory examination of the seven squares demonstrated that they differ enormously both in design characteristics and in the level of sewing skills; at least three or four different women seem to have been involved in making this group of squares (Figures 24-25). The large City Spring square in basted state and one other appliquéd square representing the Rev. John Hall of the Caroline Street Methodist Church are in the most sophisticated and elaborate Baltimore album style, but there is no specific reason to associate Mary Evans with their crafting. Perhaps she worked on one of the simpler squares in the group or on none at all. In the decades since Dr. Dunton's first explorations of the genre, numerous single squares or groups of a few incomplete squares have come to light. Their unfinished state in and of itself provides no clues to their makers. Just as visually similar squares, even within a single quilt, often show different needlework, groups of two or more incomplete squares evidence different design and stitching characteristics.

Careful examination of several hundred Baltimore album quilt squares of the most sophisticated type confirmed great consistency in design. Perhaps of equal significance, repetitive choices of the same fabrics from an enormous selection of rare and costly prints were found to be typical among squares of the same or similar designs. The same manipulations and clever conceits in fabric usage to create *trompe l'oeil* effects and three-dimensionality were also seen to be as consistent as the design characteristics and fabric selections. But at the same time, great variations in sewing techniques and qualities were obvious among designs, which were otherwise extremely similar, lending support to the idea that some quilt squares were distributed in kit or cut

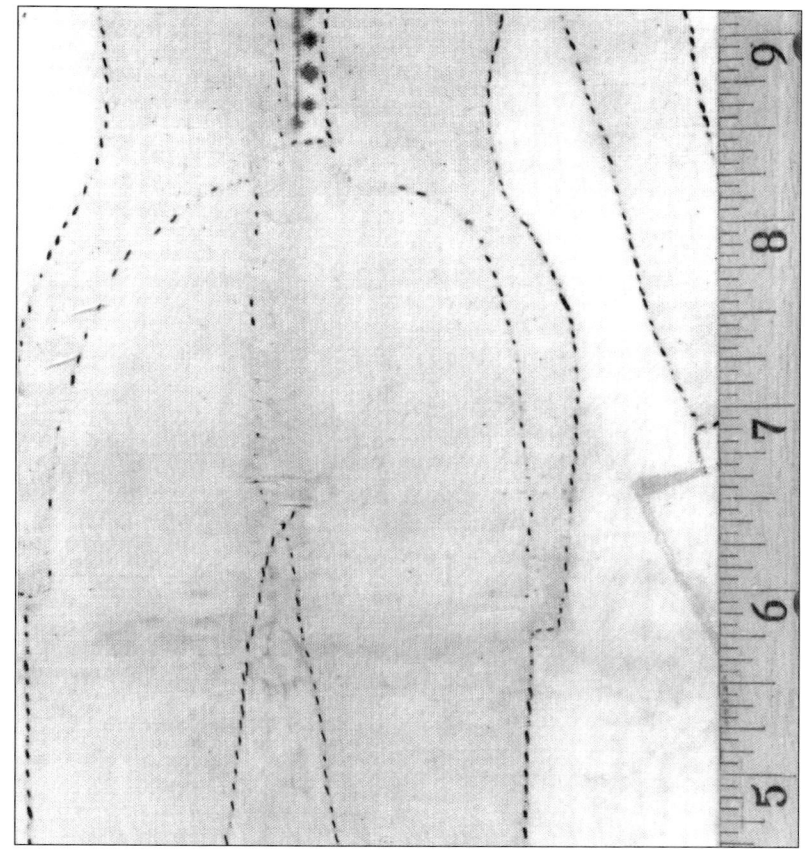

Figure 24 Detail of extremely small stitches in colored thread from back of Rev. Hall quilt square (see Catalogue 32 for front of square).

Figure 25 Detail of stitching on cornucopia square (see Catalogue 32 for front of square).

but unstitched form (Figures 26-29). Documentary evidence of kits has been sought in period newspapers and other records but has not come to light. However, small bits of what might be called circumstantial evidence have been accumulated.

For example, the Maryland Historical Society acquired an individual Ringgold Monument square (see Catalogue 33), which is inscribed:

> Sacred to/the memory of/Major Ringgold/When the gallant Ringgold received the wound/at the battle of Palo Alto, which deprived the army/of one of its brightest ornaments, some of his/comrades gathered around him, when he/intoned "Leave me to my fate there is/much for every man to do."/Cynthia Duvall/New Market/Frederick County/Maryland.

The design of the square and choice of fabrics are closely similar to at least eight other known examples.[5] All of the known Ringgold squares contain the same design anomaly in the asymmetrical arrangement of the plants and rifle fence to either side of the monument itself (Figures 30-31). This is the sort of "mistake" that could easily occur in the fast, assembly-line compilation of a group of similar kits, but is not readily explained if a carefully crafted pattern or published design description were being followed individually by different women.

The New Market square has another anomaly in the position of the eagle, which floats to the left of the monument on this square but perches on the top of the monument on other examples. If the square went out from Baltimore to New Market in loosely basted form, only one or two stitches would have had to come loose for the eagle to have fallen off. Cynthia Duvall might have simply placed it in the largest open space she could find.

Occasionally, archetypal Baltimore album quilt squares show up in quilts made in distinctly different locations and a Baltimore relative, trip, or some other connection can be established to explain how or why a Baltimore-designed square was sent elsewhere for inclusion in a quilt (Figure 32).

The extensive manuscript collections of the Maryland Historical Society yielded the following quotation, which helps substantiate the existence of basted kits and perhaps gives us the name of the woman who developed the most readily recognized, archetypal Baltimore album quilt style. On February 2, 1850, a young Baltimore Quaker woman named Hannah Mary Trimble recounted this series of visits in her diary:

1st of 2nd mo. 1850

> ...afternoon, Aunt S. & myself went to Mrs. Williams in Exeter St. to see a quilt which was being exhibited and intended for Dr. Mackenzie as a tribute of gratitude for his father's services. I could not imagine

Figure 26 Detail of appliquéd basket; compare with Figure 27 to see similar pattern, which was perhaps executed from a cut and basted kit by a different needlewoman (see Catalogue 9 for entire quilt).

Figure 27 Detail of appliquéd basket; compare with Figure 26 (see Catalogue 8 for entire quilt).

Figure 28 Detail of appliquéd basket square; compare with Figure 29. The similarity of design and fabrics may indicate that these were pre-cut kits which, were stitched and assembled into different quilts by different women (see Catalogue 7 for entire quilt).

Figure 29 Detail of appliquéd basket square; compare with Figure 28 (see Catalogue 12 for entire quilt).

any thing of the kind more perfect—it was surpassingly beautiful. The star spangled banner & holy bible—an eagle with flowers issuing out of the Liberty cap formed the center. Around it were 4 cornicopeas [sic] baskets of flowers, a great variety of wreaths &c &c &c Finished with a splendid border forming a vine and bound with shaded scarlet velvet. The quilting resembled marsales [sic]—altogether it was a magnificent piece of work. Much of it was done in buttonhole stitch and all sewn down with various shades of silk.

... then out to Mrs. Simon's in Chesnut [sic] St. The lady who cut & basted these handsome quilts—saw some pretty squares.

Next went to Mrs. Sliver's in Constitution St. and saw some very beautiful quilts, one of which was a decidedly superior one similar to Mrs. Williams—the quilting I thought prettier being done in small diamonds—the center was formed of a basket of flowers, a bible, bunches of different kinds of baskets well filled with buds & blossoms, wreaths, etc. and bound with figured scarlet chintz. I saw one the pattern of the Irish chain which was quite pretty, the next was one pattern of red & green calico—quite pretty.[6]

Almost miraculously, both the elaborate quilts seen by Miss Trimble are known today. The Williams quilt is illustrated and described in Dunton's *Old Quilts*.[7] The

Figure 30 Ringgold Monument square perhaps sent from Baltimore to New Market, Maryland, in the form of a cut and basted kit; compare with Figure 31 (see Catalogue 33).

Figure 31 Baltimore album quilt in the collection of the Abby Aldrich Rockefeller Folk Art Center, Williamsburg, Virginia. Note the Ringgold Monument Square with two flags in the top row; this square is remarkably similar to the design of the square in Figure 30 except that some ruched flowers have been substituted for more simple appliquéd ones.

Figure 32 Album quilt made in Virginia to celebrate the wedding anniversary of John and Matilda Gemeny about 1848. It is believed that the center pictorial square was sent from Baltimore by the son of the couple. Private collection.

Figure 33 Baltimore album quilt made by Mrs. Sliver, c. 1849-1850 and recorded by Hannah Mary Trimble in her diary entry for February 1, 1850. Miss Trimble's diary indicates that Mary Simon may have designed and cut out the appliqué work for this quilt. Through familiarity with this quilt, we may be able to attribute other quilts and squares to Mrs. Simon's design talents. The Baltimore Museum of Art, gift of the Friends of the American Wing, 76.93

Sliver quilt is discussed in Katzenberg's Baltimore *Album Quilts* and is now in the collection of The Baltimore Museum of Art (Figure 33).[8] These two quilts are very similar and both exemplify the finest and most elaborate design work.

Sadly, little is known about Mrs. Simon, but she is thought to have been born in 1810 in a small village named Lucktersbach in Bavaria.[9] Her name prior to her Baltimore marriage appears to have been Heidenroder; we know nothing of her background or education. Mary arrived in Baltimore in 1844 and very quickly married Philip Simon, a carpet weaver, also from Bavaria.[10] Perhaps she knew Philip before she arrived in Baltimore or met him within the close-knit German community in the city. The records of St. James Roman Catholic Church list a son Joseph born April 14, 1845, another son Adam Laurentius born October 17, 1847, a son Joannes born August 11, 1852, and a daughter Maria Theresia born November 22, 1856. It is easy to understand that creating cut and basted quilt kits would have been an acceptable and feasible way for the mother of young children to supplement the family income. The sheer quantity of squares in a consistent style and using similar fabrics precludes the likelihood that any one individual completed the appliqué work on all of them before they were distributed. The quantity of exotic fabrics in squares attributed to Mary Simon makes it highly unlikely that she, or any middle-class woman

Figure 36 Detail illustrating Mrs. Simon's characteristic use of leaf or paisley shapes on top of a flower shape to create the effect of the many petals in a three-dimensional rose (see Catalogue 7 for entire quilt).

Figure 34 Detail of pictorial square in which the idea of a three-dimensional vase is conveyed by the clever use of shaded, rainbow fabric (see Catalogue 24 for entire quilt).

Figure 35 Detail of square, which may be Mrs Simon's earlier or more "folk-y" work, or may be evidence of yet another talented designer (see Catalogue 10 for entire quilt).

could have afforded to give away or trade such costly pieces. And a careful examination of the names on entire quilts in the Mary Simon style versus those on quilts, which feature only one or a small number of her characteristic squares along with other more individualistic designs, provides a socioeconomic correlation. Indeed the names on the completely Simon-designed quilts come from a more prosperous segment of the population than those on quilts with only one of her designs.

Although it seems likely that Mary Simon composed and sold quilt square kits, she certainly would not have used the word professional, which had quite different connotations of education and status in the nineteenth century, to refer to herself. Baltimore was filled with women who supplemented or earned their living with their needles but seamstresses, milliners, tailors, and other such occupations were considered far too lowly to be called professions, and it is quite possible that Mary engaged in other work as well.

The dates of Mary Simon's arrival in Baltimore, marriage, and presumed assimilation into the local culture correspond to the emergence of the style attributed to her talents. While some Baltimore album quilt squares carry dates as early as 1842, the earliest evidence of Mary's characteristic work dates to about 1846 and she seems to have flourished during the few years between 1850 and 1854. We have not been able to determine what happened to Mary after the mid-1850s but the sudden demise of the Baltimore album style may have been hastened by her illness, death, or move westward. If the family stayed in Baltimore or simply moved elsewhere, it is somewhat surprising that her great talent did not find further expressions that can be traced.

The mature style attributed to Mary Simon is epitomized by the Horton wedding quilt (see Catalogue 7). It is characterized by a somewhat pastel palette, by elaborately layered fabrics to create complex, three-dimensional floral compositions, by a wide variety of fabrics including plain cottons and silk, small-figured calicoes, chintzes, and large-scale printed furnishing fabrics. Work attributed to Mary Simon featured inking for details and inscriptions rather than embroidery. She relied on the manipulation of shaded and rainbow fabrics rather than padding to create a sense of three-dimensionality (Figure 34). The famous, intricately woven red baskets, miniature figures in fully tailored garments, and most pictorial landscape, monument, and ship squares may be attributed to Mary Simon (see Catalogue 7-12, 21, 23, 24). Slightly more stylized designs using a great deal of brilliant blue rainbow fabric with applied yellow and red accents may represent a

Figure 37 Detail of square showing flat flowers with wool blanket-stitched edges and embroidered centers (see Catalogue 16 for entire quilt).

Figure 38 Detail of square showing stuffed flowers with inlaid appliquéd centers in same design and from the same quilt as the square in Figure 37. The differences in technique seem to imply that two different women stitched squares cut from the same pattern. (see Catalogue 16 for entire quilt).

Figure 39 Detail of red lyre square, c. 1850; compare with Figure 40 (see Catalogue 26 for entire quilt).

Figure 40 Detail of red lyre square (compare with Figure 39), which may have been made from the same pattern or cut by the same designer as others. Differences in such simplified squares may be due to the various tastes and skills of the needlewomen (see Catalogue 27 for entire quilt).

slightly more "folk-y" phase of her work or that of another, similar, very talented designer (Figure 35). It also appears that Mary Simon may have experimented with reverse or inlaid appliquéd flowers before developing her characteristic layered leaf or paisley-shaped petal technique (Figure 36).

The distinctive characteristics of several other designers may also be discerned among the body of surviving Baltimore album quilts along with individualistic designs and adaptations. None of the names of these other talented women are known as yet.

Designer II's work relied on a strongly red-and-green color scheme, additional padding or ruching to create dimension, and quantities of wool and silk embroidery for details and highlights; there is little or no inking on Designer II quilt squares (see Catalogue 15, 16). A number of Designer II quilts have sashing and/or borders of red-and-white appliquéd triangles (see Catalogue 15). It has become apparent that many Designer II quilt squares predate the work of Mary Simon, and Designer II quilt designs are less complex than many attributed to Mrs. Simon. Designer II featured fewer fabrics in general and more plain fabrics than Mrs. Simon used, and Designer II quilts often closely resemble Pennsylvania quilts in their boldness. Designer II rarely layered fabric pieces but occasionally used inlaid or reverse appliqué over fabric inserts. Her roses, made of a single piece of cloth, were defined by embroidered outlines for petals and satin-stitched highlights. Like Mrs. Simon's oeuvre, some quilts seem to have been entirely designed and laid out by Designer II while other quilts combine some Designer II squares with squares by other artists. Designer II is the only Baltimore album quilt designer besides Mary Simon whose work survives in enough quantity that similarities in fabric selection but definite differences in technical execution can clearly be discerned among similar designs (Figures 37-38). These factors may indicate that Designer II also produced kits or patterns of some sort.

A group of at least eight known quilts represent the unusual and witty work of Designer III.[1] This third artist deliberately stylized flowers rather than striving for naturalism. Her flowers closely resemble the exotic printed and embroidered Persian, Indian, and Chinese textiles that inspired eighteenth-century crewel-embroidered bed hangings (see Catalogue 18). On the other hand, Designer III was fascinated by animals and lavishly deployed both domestic and outlandish animals across her quilts. Designer III had a very personal and modern approach to fabric and color selection using black velvet for a horse, grey tweed for an elephant, and combining such colors as orchid and apricot for a blossom. Her work was less inclined to use printed calico than the designs attributed to Mary Simon, but Designer III was more willing to experiment with non-traditional quilting fabrics.

The symbolic content of both Designer II's and Designer III's work is dominated by Mexican War references, which help date many of these quilts to the late 1840s before Mary Simon's style became preeminent. Like Designer II, Designer III exploited lavish embroidery for texture and details rather than the super-refined inking, which may have been part of Mary Simon's own handiwork or that of a close associate since it primarily appears on squares attributed to her design.

There were undoubtedly other talented women whose designs and quilt squares inspired and influenced the work of others. Our lack of recognition may be due to the accidental survival of some quilts but not others, or the work of some designers may appear so frequently that the personal distinctions have been submerged in the amazing quantity of Baltimore album quilts that are known today. Certainly, there are a number of less sophisticated, more stylized designs, which appear over and over again. In many instances, the red lyre squares, nine-blossom asymmetrical sprays, leafy reel, and other designs are so similar from quilt to quilt that they may have been cut from the same patterns and streamlined or elaborated as a specific needlewoman's skills and taste dictated (Figures 39-40).

At least three very large quilts with a central medallion plan share characteristics that may indicate the efforts of yet another designer (see Catalogue 22). The enormous sizes, medallion plans, and largely red-and-green color schemes of these quilts point to dates in the early or mid-1840s. Although the appliqué work is so delicate as to be feathery or wispy in character, the quilts share a crowded, chaotic appearance, which may indicate a lack of familiarity with the design discipline inherent in the organization of regular squares in a grid.

While there is some evidence that Mary Simon distributed at least some of her designs as cut and basted squares, we have no evidence about the method by which other designs were disseminated. Despite concerted searches, no advertisements or public mention of quilt patterns, templates, or kits from this period in Baltimore have been found. Nor have paper or cloth patterns or models been located. The individual squares that survive appear to be too carefully constructed and worked to have been models in the same way that some basted-together pieced squares are thought to have served as patterns (see Catalogue 32, 33).[12] Perhaps other designers also made up and sold kits; perhaps some gave out or traded designs among friends and associates; perhaps some extraordinary needle artists simply inspired others to copy their finished work closely.

After considering the wide variety of designs and techniques that appear on these quilts, identifying the characteristics of at least three distinctive major designers, and finding a number of quilts from the Harford County and northern Maryland as well as southern Pennsylvania area, the question of what constitutes a Baltimore album quilt again arises. It is often difficult to determine just where a particular quilt was made and, in fact, numerous quilts provide evidence that their squares were made in a variety of locations for assembly elsewhere. One might consider that having a Mary Simon, Designer II, or Designer III square would identify a quilt as of Baltimore origin, but it has been found that these squares were undoubtedly sometimes sent out from the city center for completion and inclusion in quilts elsewhere. In addition, there are many quilts with strong Baltimore histories, which have none of the characteristic designer squares that have so far been identified. In other words, some non-Baltimore City quilts look highly sophisticated and some Baltimore-made quilts are simplified and stylized interpretations of the style. To complicate the matter further, there are a few quilts, which are clearly in one of the major designer's style, but which are not technically album quilts, being either whole cloth or center medallion in format.

Perhaps at this point it is wisest to beg the question and include all quilts known to have been made in Baltimore; all quilts with a Mary Simon, Designer II, or Designer III feature; and all quilts that closely resemble these and which, from their style, fabrics, and histories have a good chance of having been made in Maryland under the influence of Baltimore needlewomen between about 1842 and 1862.

Why Were Baltimore Album Quilts Made?

The more we study the phenomenon of mid-nineteenth-century Baltimore album quilts, the more similar the motivations, reasons, and methodology of their original creators seem to those of fine quiltmakers today. Baltimore album quilts were made for very special reasons. Hannah Mary Trimble's diary and reports of the Maryland Institute Fairs recount the deliberate exhibition of extraordinary Baltimore album quilts as works of textile art.

In 1848, the Maryland Institute for the Promotion of the Mechanic Arts began a series of enormous annual fairs. This was a local phase of the massive international exposition movement, which culminated in such events as the great Crystal Palace exhibition of 1851 in London and the Paris Exposition of 1889. The Maryland Institute Fairs included competitive categories with judges and prizes for every imaginable industrial and home product. Entries came from across the state and beyond, and the fairs were heavily attended by fashionable Baltimoreans and visitors from a wide area. The fair opened about the beginning of October and ran until the beginning of November; diaries indicate that it was the place to be seen during its duration, and many courting couples took advantage of the opportunity for several outings (Figure 41).

The fairs were reported in enormous detail in the local press and published reports by the organizers and judges were circulated. Frustratingly, the lists of items exhibited are too brief for us to imagine what the items looked like; they give only the name of the exhibitor and the most cursory description such as "fancy quilt," "album quilt," "mathematical star quilt," and even, curiously, "knitted" and "crochet quilt." Nevertheless, the reports permit us to track the relative popularity of types of handwork. Between 1850 and 1853, the number of quilts shown remained fairly steady at about 150, but by 1854, wool needlepoint--then called worsted work or, later, Berlin work--and white eyelet-type embroidery were definitely in the ascendancy.[13]

Local newspaper references show that, while it lasted, the fine Baltimore quilt fad of the mid-nineteenth century was admired and appreciated by the culture that spawned it. Newspaper accounts indicate that Baltimore women publicly displayed quilts made for national figures:

Quilt for Henry Clay...The Clay quilt, which we noticed a few days ago, has been placed at Mr. Butcher's, in Charles street, where persons desirous of seeing it may call from 10 till 5 today, and from 10 till 12 tomorrow.

The Baltimore American, September 19, 1845. In addition to the Maryland Institute Fair reports, the local newspapers took notice of the finest quilts, which were displayed there:

Fair of the Maryland Institute...Cincinnati star quilt composed of an infinitesimal number of pieces of calico tastefully and judiciously arranged in the form of a large star, by Miss M. Parks, of Baltimore, who deposits besides a splendid album quilt, elaborately worked and both highly creditable to the taste and industry of the fair fabricatrix.

Baltimore Republican & Argus, October 3, 1849. And when Baltimore quilts were exhibited as far away as Washington, D.C., local newspapermen resorted to quoting from the Capital City newspapers to describe the praise heaped on these products of Baltimore female ingenuity:

A Splendid specimen of Baltimore Skill. a Washington paper, speaking of the interesting and beautiful deposits in the Exhibition of the Metropolitan Institute, now open at the Federal City [Washington, D.C.], in the large and spacious Hall of the Smithsonian Institute [sic], refers to a splendid specimen of Baltimore handy-work in the following complimentary terms: "The second article is a superb quilt, made by Mrs. Fowler, of Baltimore, and is a most magnificent affair. Four American flags, with tassels ornament the quilt, worked in silk, and two eagles with America's shield, are worked at either side. It is of the most exquisite manufacture,

Figure 41 Illustration of the Maryland Institute Fair from *The Monumental City* by John C. Gobright, published by Gobright & Torsch, 1858; pp. 66-67.

and an honor to the hand and heart of the lady contributing it."

Baltimore Republican & Argus, February 9, 1855. In addition to providing acceptable avenues by which needle artists could show off their accomplishments, many Baltimore album quilts were made as gifts to mark major life events. Of all quilts known to have been made for presentation, by far the largest number were made as gifts to church ministers, especially those moving to new assignments or going west as missionaries (see Catalogue 25, 31, 32).

A number of Baltimore album quilts have been handed down with a family tradition that they were freedom quilts made to celebrate a young man's twenty-first birthday or the date at which he completed his apprenticeship and became free to hire himself out or establish his own business (see Catalogue 23, 29).

The term Baltimore Bride's quilt seems to be a euphonious phrase of recent coinage. Surprisingly few Baltimore album quilts can be documented to the time of a wedding, although they are often the most exquisite examples of the genre (see Catalogue 7). Several were created to honor important wedding anniversaries. A small number of red-and-green album crib quilts have been found in the Baltimore area, but no quilts incorporating the most elaborate or pictorial type of Baltimore appliqué squares have been located that were made for infants or children.

The inscriptions, which form such a fascinating aspect of many Baltimore album quilts, provide vital evidence of kin and friendship groups, which may be traced today by researching the names through the census, maps, genealogical, church, and fraternal organization records.

Where Did The Designs On Baltimore Album Quilts Come From And What Do They Mean?

Baltimore album quilts are justly famous for the range of fabrics they exhibit and the exceptional needlework they present, but the designs in the squares are unquestionably the most astonishing features of these national heirlooms. Today we are so bombarded with visual stimulation that it is difficult to envision how little imagery was available to the women who made Baltimore album quilts. Not only were there no movies or televisions, no gorgeously illustrated "coffee table" books or magazines as we know them, but even the colorful and graphically powerful packaging for food and household products, which confronts us every time we open cupboard doors, was nonexistent. Photography was in the very earliest stages of its development, and decorated home furnishings were far less available and far more expensive than they are today. Without classes or published patterns, Baltimore's quiltmakers of one hundred fifty years ago reached deep into their own experiences and creativity to produce these unique works of textile art.

Unquestionably, many quiltmakers used their formal educations as resources. The decorative graduation samplers of the 1830s, when many of the quilters were in their teens and were finishing their sojourns at female academies, exhibit many of the most popular quilt designs--baskets and bouquets of flowers, frontally composed buildings and landmarks, exotic and symbolic fruit like the pineapple (Figure 42). Silk- embroidered mourning pictures provided models for monuments and clues as to how trees, water, and landscape features might be rendered in cloth (Figure 43). Theorem paintings on velvet inspired similar compositions in fabric; specifically, nearly identical, shaded blue *compotiers* with cut watermelons and other fruit appear in both mediums. Treasured album books provided sketched motifs and verses to be reproduced in ink on quilts.

Printed textiles themselves, especially chintzes, were perhaps the most immediate models for many quilt designs. In fact, reproducing the effect of floral chintz may have been the motivation behind the development of the most intricately layered floral appliquéd squares and borders. The most popular designs—baskets, vases, wreaths, swags of full-blown blossoms, exotic birds, *compotiers* of fruit, even animals, buildings, and other patterns—could have been directly translated from contemporary or slightly older chintz fabrics.

Quite likely, the idea of including scenes on a quilt was transferred from earlier printed toiles; a late eighteenth-century French toile made into a bedspread in the collection of The Copper Lantern, Inc. shop illustrates a woman milking a cow.[14] Even the ducks in the foreground of the printed fabric appear appliquéd in a nearly identical scene on some Baltimore album quilts. This is not the sort of design a woman might be expected to execute on an appliquéd quilt without some sort of perceived authorization that it was an appropriate textile motif. A chintz fabric in a quilt at the Philadelphia Museum of Art includes a hunter and dogs virtually identical to those on some Baltimore album quilts.[15] And formal buildings form important elements in neoclassical fabrics, just as textiles, carpets, wallpapers, and other decorative arts of the first quarter of the nineteenth-century abound in Roman architectural rosette designs which may have inspired or validated many of the cut-paper patterns on quilts. In addition to very specific design details, the chintz quilts of the gentry from previous decades quite obviously provided the models for what middle-class women thought a fancy quilt should look like.

The small, standard printers' cuts, which were used as space fillers and vaguely relevant illustrations in newspapers and broadsides, provided easily copied, linear designs. The 1854 catalogue of printers' ready-made type published by the Baltimore Type Company shows almost every design to be found on Baltimore album quilts.[16] Of particular interest, since they might have been less available elsewhere, are the designs for various organizational and patriotic insignia. Among other quite direct precedents for quilt patterns are the depictions of the U. S. Capitol Building in Washington, D. C., and even a fashionably dressed man obviously intended for use in tailors' notices—the clothing and pose are especially similar to several figures identified on quilt squares as Methodist ministers (Figures 44-45). This catalogue of small illustrations even includes a Mexican War soldier with a flag like the figure on the quilt designated Catalogue 10. In addition, there are Irish harps, a lady riding sidesaddle, a hunting scene with a man and dog posed like those on several quilts, and up-to-the-minute steamboats, sailing ships, trains, and fire-fighting equipment.

More elaborate engravings printed on billheads, currency, newspaper mastheads, and as frontispieces or illustrations in books occasionally were reproduced on quilts. For example, a particularly jaunty horse and rider, which appears on two different Designer III quilts, has been traced to page 213 of an 1848 Philadelphia-published book called *Pictorial History of Mexico and the Mexican War* by John Frost, LL.D. (Figures 46-47). The symbolic motifs associated with the several fraternal organizations represented on Baltimore album quilts were probably available to quiltmakers from ornate membership certificates and fancy gift books published for members (see below).

Some motifs such as baskets of flowers and wreaths were so much part of the culture of the day that they

Figure 42 Flower basket sampler, Baltimore, 1830; made by Fany [sic] Bush in 1830 at St. James First African Protestant Episcopal Church School, Baltimore. This sampler is in the elaborate English tradition; the design of a basket of flowers was ubiquitous on needlework, printed textiles, and all other forms of decorative and domestic arts at this time. The Emilie McKim Reed Memorial Purchase Fund, 89.29.2

Figure 43 Silk-embroidered mourning picture probably worked by Louisa Davis (1824-1868) at St. Joseph's Academy, near Emmitsburg, Maryland, c. 1839. Gift of Mrs. Thomas Chew Worthington, 53.143.1

Figure 44 Detail of appliqué square depicting the Rev. Hall of the Caroline Street Methodist Church, c. 1850 (see Catalogue 32). The design for such squares may have been inspired or influenced by simple printers' cuts such as that shown in Figure 45.

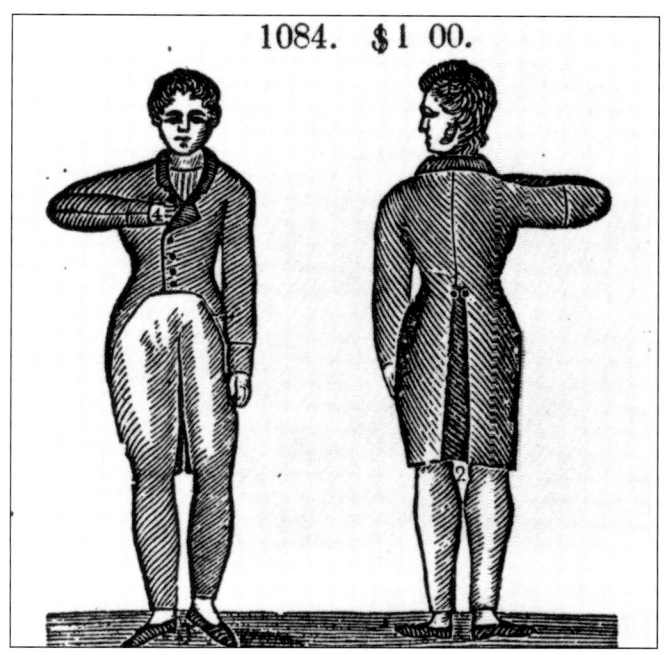

Figure 45 Cut number 1084 from *Specimens of Printing Types and Ornaments Cast at the Baltimore Type and Stereotype Foundry*, published by Lucas Brothers in Baltimore in 1854. Note that some items in this catalogue would have been available for widespread use at a considerably earlier date.

appear in nearly identical form on silver, woven and printed furnishing fabrics, wallpaper, carved or painted furniture, dishes, and many other artifacts. Stylized, non-pictorial designs also were part of the general visual vocabulary.

It is a delightful game to find the similarities between images on Baltimore album quilts and objects in common circulation such as glass flasks, daguerreotype frames, political and organizational badges, sheet music, calling cards, etc. We invariably find that the "pictures" that made their way onto quilts represented the most fashionable and topical material of the day. There was nothing quaint or nostalgic about these quilts at the time they were made. The buildings and monuments were the newest and most important. The ships, trains, trolleys, and fire engines represented the latest inventions. Even the hymns, poems, and religious sentiments of the inscriptions were the most current.

The more one looks, the more one finds Mexican War imagery on Baltimore album quilts, especially those with characteristics of Designers II and III. These images may be as overt as depictions of uniformed officers and soldiers, military encampments or operations, and monuments and inscriptions to particular heroes, or as subtle as general patriotic and national emblems or portrayals of varieties of cacti which were introduced from Mexico at this time as stylish houseplants.

Probably one sort of thing which had an enormous impact on how Baltimore album quilt squares looked was transfer-printed Staffordshire dishes, which came into the port of Baltimore in enormous quantity during the mid-nineteenth century. For the first time, high quality, decorative crockery was readily available in quantity and at reasonable cost to ordinary, middle-class American housewives. These dishes represented a giant step in refinement from previously obtainable plain cream ware, coarse redware pottery and wooden vessels. Understandably, the appetite for Staffordshire ware was inexhaustible. It was so popular that wily English manufacturers and distributors created designs for the American market and even specifically for Baltimore. The transfer-printed technique for ceramic decoration reduced designs to their linear, two-dimensional components which were easily copied by quilt fabricators. The central design—whether building, ship, legendary figures, or ornamental composition—usually was surrounded on Staffordshire plates by a floral border in a large scale unrelated to the scale of the center. This is exactly the format reiterated hundreds

Figure 46 Detail of cavalryman square on Baltimore album quilt, c. 1849 (see Catalogue 19 for entire quilt).

and hundreds of times on Baltimore album quilt squares. Other plates employed other borders or elements--zigzag, drapery swags, fruit garlands—which also became such a common part of the visual culture that they appear frequently on Baltimore album quilts. At a time when it would have been socially unacceptable, even unimaginable, for a woman to sit outdoors in public to sketch a major urban building or monument (and certainly not on the docks to draw a ship!), she could find them already delineated within a suitable border just inside her pantry cupboard (Figures 48-51).

Among Staffordshire patterns were those designed with emblems to appeal to members of the popular fraternal organizations such as the Freemasons, the Independent Order of Odd Fellows, and various agricultural, temperance, and political societies (Figure 52). These show up with great regularity on Baltimore album quilts because most quilts were made as gifts for men (see above), and the 1840s and 1850s were the heyday of fraternal organizations. In particular, the Independent Order of Odd Fellows, established in late-eighteenth-century England as a workingman's mutual aid society, was first introduced to America by way of Baltimore in 1819.[17] By 1850, the local membership was not only enormous, but highly influential. Significantly, agitation to include women as Odd

Figure 47 Illustration of Captain Walker on page 213 of *Pictorial History of Mexico and the Mexican War* by John Frost, LL.D., published in Philadelphia in 1848.

Figure 48 Imported English Staffordshire transfer-printed plate for the American market. Note the swag border listing the fifteen states in the Union. Made by James and Ralph Clews, Cobridge, England, c. 1830. Bequest of Josephine Cushing Morris, 56.50.139

Figure 49 Imported English Staffordshire transfer-printed plate depicting the Baltimore Merchants' Exchange surrounded by a floral wreath-like border. Made by Henshall and Co. of Burslem, England, c. 1835. Gift of Edward Hopper, 56.35.1

Figure 50 Imported English Staffordshire transfer-printed plate depicting the Baltimore Battle Monument within a floral border. Made by J. & J. Jackson, Burslem, England, c. 1840. Private Collection.

Figure 51 Imported English Staffordshire transfer-printed plate perhaps depicting the "all-seeing eye" and dove of the Odd Fellows. Note the sawtooth or zigzag border such as appears on many quilts. Unknown maker; pattern named "Millenium," England, c. 1845. Private collection.

Figure 52 English jug bearing the importers mark of Clark, Levering and Co., Baltimore, c. 1845. The motifs are all symbols of the Independent Order of Odd Fellows. Gift of Sumpter Priddy, 87.81

Fellows began in 1845, and women were admitted to limited membership in 1851.[18] The three-link chain standing for "Friendship, Love, Truth", the red, yellow, and blue colors also emblematic of those principles, the all-seeing eye, and the busy beehive are motifs that recur on quantities of Baltimore album quilts. In fact, there has been speculation that the three-loop bow so characteristic of many Baltimore album quilt designs may be a discrete form of feminine I.O.O.F. three-link chain.[19]

Freemasonry had been especially popular among eighteenth-century intellectuals, and its principles and symbolism played important roles in the establishment of the United States. George Washington, Benjamin Franklin, Lafayette, John Hancock and many of the "Founding Fathers" were members of Masonic lodges.

A number of agricultural societies were established in Maryland during the 1840s and 1850s with the goal of improving agriculture through scientific methods and new inventions. The Maryland Farmer's Club was founded in Baltimore in 1845; this was replaced in 1848 by the Maryland Agricultural and Mechanical Association. The first State Agricultural Fair was held in early November 1848 under the auspices of The State Agricultural Society.

Temperance organizations also gained members and clout as the century progressed. The Temperance

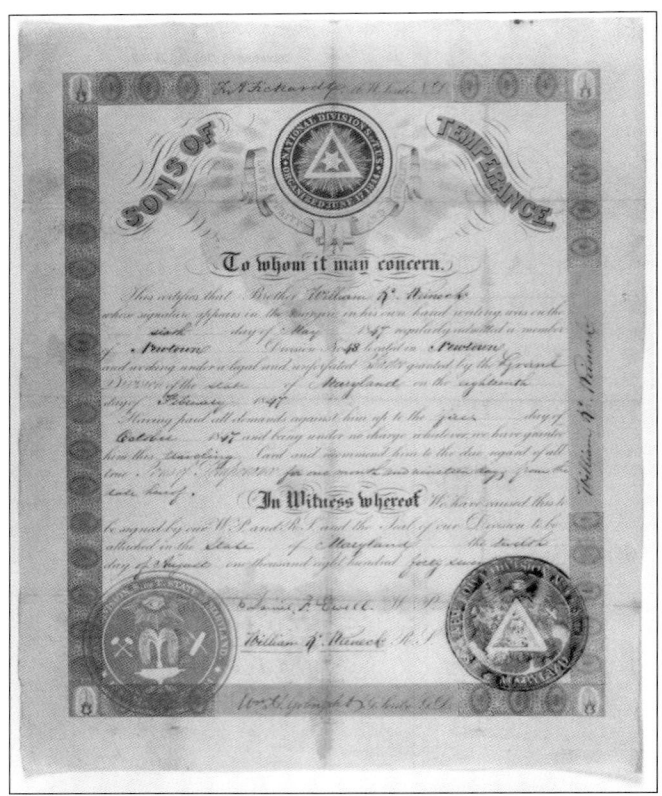

Figure 53 Sons of Temperance certificate with the triangular motif and Fountain of Life design found on Baltimore album quilts. Division of Prints and Photographs, Maryland Historical Society, Purchase, 1932.

Society established various branches throughout the state in 1831, but the most important such group locally was the Sons of Temperance founded in 1844 (Figure 53). Sons of Temperance motifs such as the six-pointed star within a triangle and the "fountain of life" (pure water) often appeared on Baltimore album quilts (Figure 54).

Organizational symbols are present on nearly all Baltimore album quilts. However, since many symbols were used by more than one organization, it is sometimes difficult to determine which group was intended. For example, the "all-seeing eye" representing the all-knowing power of God was used by the Masons, the Odd Fellows, the Sons of Temperance, and the United States government (it still appears at the top of the pyramid on the back of the one dollar bill). Similarly, crossed keys were used to indicate both secrecy and the office of treasurer by many groups. Some symbols, like the bee skip or hive to indicate industriousness, were used by so many groups, including the Maryland Institute itself, that they may have entered an almost universal or common code of symbolism and been used sometimes without any direct affiliation with a specific organization.

One of the most curious symbols to occur on several Baltimore album quilts is the log-cabin-and-cider-barrel motif developed by the Harrison-Tyler ticket during the 1840 Presidential campaign (Figure 55).

Figure 55 Whig Party log-cabin-and-cider-barrel symbol from Baltimore album quilt, c. 1845-1848 (see Catalogue 23 for entire quilt).

Figure 54 Sons of Temperance square from Baltimore album quilt, 1846-1847 (see Catalogue 25 for entire quilt).

Figure 56 Frontispiece from 1838 edition of *Flora's Dictionary* by Mrs. Elizabeth Wirt, published by Fielding Lucas, Jr., in Baltimore.

The design was instigated by Harrison's political opponents as a slur on his ambitions, but Harrison brilliantly turned the tables by claiming it referred to his background as a "common man." Harrison died very soon after taking office; the log-cabin-end-cider-barrel motif was used again during Henry Clay's unsuccessful 1844 bid for the presidency. During the 1840 and 1844 campaigns, this motif was used on badges, ribbons, printed fabric, even drinking glasses and other souvenirs. These items certainly were still around years later and the design may have been copied from them onto quilts without any conscious reference to a political meaning. It is highly unlikely that the quilt squares date as early as the campaigns themselves.

This was an era and culture intrigued by visual symbolism. Between 1838 and 1855, Mrs. Elizabeth W. Wirt's *Flora's Dictionary*, a highly imaginative directory of floral symbolism or the language of flowers, went through three editions published by Fielding Lucas, Jr., in Baltimore alone (Figure 56). Similar gift books by other authors were also published locally, in Philadelphia, and in other centers throughout the English-speaking world. Unquestionably, flowers and other motifs as sentimental symbols were prevalent and popular, but each author or publisher seems to have developed his own set of meanings. Obviously the language of flowers was not a rigid code that anyone took seriously. A red rose might mean one thing to one person one day and something else to another person another day. To some quilters, a red rose might simply have been a way to show off fashionable and brilliant cloth. Just as quiltmakers today often associate their choices of colors, fabrics, and designs with deeply personal significance, so probably did quiltmakers of the past, but it is pure speculation to try to reconstruct much of those private meanings 150 years later.

What Techniques Were Used On Baltimore Album Quilts?

In an elegiac sense, Baltimore album quilts may qualify as the last great burst of artistic energy expressed exclusively through hand sewing. Although 1846 is the year in which a practical sewing machine was invented, this miracle of technology was not widely available for home use for at least another decade. The earliest Baltimore newspaper advertisement for a sewing machine was probably in 1854, just as the Baltimore album quilt style was waning. During the album quilt craze, Maryland women were still responsible for sewing all bedding, towels, table linen, children's clothing, husband's clothing, their own clothing, and that of any servants or slaves. Letters and diaries abound with comments on the never-diminished mountain of sewing and mending. Certainly women in more prosperous households had skilled servants and slaves to help and could bring in talented hired seamstresses for weeks at a time to produce fashionable clothing for the family. It is likely that many of the women who indulged in making Baltimore album quilts had sewing helpers who took on the routine chores so that the lady or daughters of the house could devote time to the fine needlework of which they were so proud. Mid-nineteenth-century Baltimore was a center for early "manufactured" or ready-to-wear clothing, but in 1850, most of it was still being made as piecework by people sewing at home; for example, there was no men's shirt manufacturer, in the modern sense of the word, in Baltimore until 1858.[20]

Baltimore album quilts are technical masterpieces.

Among the needlework techniques used to enhance these textiles are traditional appliqué of intricate and delicate shapes, reverse and inlaid appliqué, layered appliqué, interwoven appliqué strips, gathered appliqué, ruching, stuffed work, cording, and piping. In many instances, the appliqué is worked with white thread; in other cases, colored thread closely matching the appliqué fabric helped hide the diminutive stitches. Most appliqué work on Baltimore album quilts was done with the relatively invisible appliqué stitch favored today; some stitchers, however, preferred buttonhole, blanket, chain, or other more obvious, decorative embroidery stitches to hold the cloth pieces together. The quality of stitching varied considerably from merely passable to almost microscopically fine.

The appliqué work was enhanced in many cases by elaborate embroidery, watercolor painting, and ink drawings and inscriptions. Colors, fabric selections, and textural contrasts were carefully considered to enhance the realistic, three-dimensional quality of these works of textile art. Because of the visual and textural richness of Baltimore album quilts, many were quilted in rather simple, albeit finely executed, quilting patterns.

What Do Baltimore Album Quilts Tell Us About The Women Who Made Them?

Baltimore album quilts may be studied as cultural and historical documents. Evidence provided by Baltimore album quilts contradicts or enlarges some of the popular beliefs about all American quilts and the lives of all Victorian women. Although we have been able to learn little about most of the women as individuals, study of the quilts in the Maryland Historical Society collection and consideration of more than 300 additional Baltimore album quilts through either direct examination or photographs have led to a number of conclusions.

Most surviving Baltimore album quilts have never been washed and show no damage from wear—disintegrated fabric is usually due to the action over time of harsh dyes or mordants, which have caused the fibers to self-destruct; brown stains are usually from long contact during storage with acidic paper or wood.

Baltimore album quilts generally have little or no batting. These facts provide evidence that these quilts were not made for use as warm bedding; these quilts were made as extravagant gifts and examples of self-expression to be used occasionally for decorative purposes. In fact, the display of these quilts only two or three times a year during very special occasions must have taken on almost ritualistic overtones, just as the use of a specific tablecloth for Thanksgiving dinner year after year might today. Baltimore album quilts were made of new and expensive fabrics rather than of discarded scraps or used materials. Evidently, the hundreds of women who were involved in making Baltimore album quilts had considerable money at their personal disposal to spend on non-essentials. So much attention has been paid to the necessarily frugal quilters of the western frontier that the myth of "make do" has attached itself firmly to American quilts. In fact, quilting started in this country as a refined pastime for those with ample luxury goods, and Baltimore album quilts were devised, at least in part, as ways of replicating the effects of highly fashionable and exorbitantly expensive furnishing textiles.

The surviving large number of fine Baltimore album quilts, each representing thousands of hours of work completed within a decade or less, indicates that middle-class women also had substantial leisure time to devote to artistic and extravagant pursuits. And that they could spend that time indulging their own tastes and proclivities.

The patriotic, political, and other current topics depicted on Baltimore album quilts reveal that the women of Baltimore were not the shy, retiring females obsessed with "children, kitchen, church" of Victorian story, but were aware citizens, despite their lack of civil rights. The quilts contain subtle and direct commentaries on political choices, major world events, the evils of alcohol, the benefits of charitable and various other aid associations, the advantages of modern inventions, the perceived rewards of regular church attendance, etc. These quilts were made by women whose lives were more similar to our own in many ways than their experiences were to those of their sisters and cousins who lived in more rural areas or who participated in the great westward expansion. The surviving quilts stimulated us to look more deeply into these women's lives and expectations, as recounted in the following essay.

NOTES
1 Semmes, *Baltimore As Seen by Visitors*, 1783-1860, 140-141.
2 de Dillmont, *Encyclopedia of Needlework*, 195-206.
3 For two points of view see Suellen Meyer, "Characteristics of Missouri-German Quilts," in *Uncoverings 1984*, ed. Sally Garoutte (San Francisco: American Quilt Study Group, 1985), 100-111. And Elizabeth Weyrauch Shea and Patricia Cox Crews, "Nebraska Quiltmakers 1870-1940," in *Uncoverings 1989*, 150.
4 For discussions of the Mary Evans' theories see Orlofsky, *Quilts in America*, 239 (1974 edition) or 255 (1992 edition) which seems to be the first widely available reference that mentions Mary Evans outside of Dunton's notes in the collection of The Baltimore Museum of Art; see also Katzenberg, *Baltimore Album Quilts*, 53, 61-62; Sienkiewicz, "The Marketing of Mary Evans" in *Uncoverings 1989*, 7 -24.
5 Baltimore album quilts with Ringgold Memorial squares may be seen in the collections of The Shelburne Museum, Vermont, the Abby Aldrich Rockefeller Folk Art Center, Williamsburg, Virginia, and several private collections, as well as in the individual square and a quilt in the Maryland Historical Society collection.
6 Hannah Mary Trimble Papers, MS 2517. Manuscripts Division, Maryland Historical Society, diary entry of 1 February 1850.
7 Dunton, *Old Quilts*, 34-43.
8 Katzenberg, *Baltimore Album Quilts*, 106.
9 Entry for: Philip Simon. P381, 8th Ward, Baltimore, Maryland, 1850 Census.
10 Ibid.
11 These include two quilts and a number of squares on a third quilt in the Maryland Historical Society collection, a quilt at The Shelburne Museum, Vermont, and a number of quilts in private collections.
12 Barbara Brackman, lecture presented at the Maryland Historical Society, November 12, 1993.
13 *Third Annual Exhibition of the Maryland Institute for the Promotion of the Mechanic Arts, Held October 14th 1850, at Washington Hall, Baltimore* (Baltimore: Printed by Sherwood & Co., 1850; *The Book Of the Exhibition. Fourth Annual Exhibition of the Maryland Institute* (Baltimore: Printed by John Murphy & Co., 1851); *The Book of the Exhibition. Fifth Annual Exhibition of the Maryland Institute* (Baltimore: From the Press of Sands & Mills, 1852); *The Book of the Exhibition. Sixth Annual Exhibition of the Maryland Institute for the Promotion of the Mechanic Arts* (Baltimore: From the Press of Sands & Mills, 1853); *The Book of the Exhibition. Seventh Annual Exhibition of the Maryland Institute for the Promotion of the Mechanic Arts* (Baltimore: From the Press of Sands & Mills, 1854).
14 The Copper Lantern, Inc., Old Greenwich, CT, advertisement, *Antiques and The Arts Weekly*, July 29, 1994, 97.
15 Blum and Lindsey, *Nineteenth-Century Applique Quilts* (Bulletin, vol. 85, numbers 363-364; Philadelphia Museum of Art, Fall 1989), 14-15.
16 ..... *Specimens of Printing Types and Ornaments Cast at the Baltimore Type and Stereotype Foundry* (Baltimore: Lucas Brothers, 1854).
17 ..... *An Account of the Grand Celebration of the Independent Order of Odd-Fellows* (Baltimore, Sands & Neilson, 1831), 10-22.
18 I.O.O.F. records state that in 1851 the wives, daughters, mothers and sisters of Odd Fellows were admitted to membership in the Rebekah Degree. However, Rebekah Lodges were not officially established in Maryland until 1886 with the Colfax Lodge No. 1 in Cumberland, Maryland, and Queen Esther Lodge No. 2 in Baltimore ("Maryland Rebekahs," in *Baltimore Evening Sun*, 5 January 1951). This delay seems curious in light of the very large and active membership in the I.O.O.F. in the state. Nevertheless, other Baltimore-made decorative arts besides album quilts show evidence of the excitement the Rebekah Degree caused among the female population. In particular, the most popular product of the famous Edwin Bennett pottery, first introduced about 1851-1852 and in continuous production into the 1930s, was a brown-glazed teapot with a molded depiction of the Biblical Rebekah at the Well. Significantly, the teapot used the same spelling for the name as used by the Odd Fellows, although there are several more common alternative spellings.
19 Elly Sienkiewicz, lecture presented at the Maryland Historical Society, 17 June 1994.
20 Kahn, Philip, Jr. A Stitch in Time: *The Four Seasons Of Baltimore's Needle Trades*, 38.

Domestic Spheres And Home Circles:
The Dimensions Of Early-Nineteenth-Century Baltimore Women's Lives

by Barbara K. Weeks

Many of the women who designed, cut, basted, and quilted Baltimore album quilts left their names inked or cross-stitched on their squares so that we have a simplistic answer to the question "who made these quilts?" But far larger questions intrigue those who study the quilts: how do these textiles reflect the lives of the individuals who stitched them, and how do they represent the time and place in which they were crafted? It became clear that an understanding of early-nineteenth-century events, both local and national, as well as knowledge of women's lives, was vital to an informed understanding of the quilts. This story should not be one stereotyped in our twentieth-century attitudes, but rather needed to come from period sources. I read a vast number of early- to mid-nineteenth-century documents to acquire a sense of the period. These writings included women's letters and diaries, albums and commonplace books, ladies' magazines, novels, poetry, and gift books. Health department reports, newspapers, cookbooks, and conduct books--in short, anything written by or for women, contributed a perspective on the experience of antebellum Baltimore women.

Because most of the women who left a written record were from the middle or upper classes and because much of the advice written for women was directed to this same group, information about these women is relatively abundant. These women had both the leisure time and education to record thoughts in diaries; they had the time to invest in appliquéing and quilting the principally decorative Baltimore album quilts. We have learned through genealogical research that most of the women whose names appear on quilt squares were part of what would now be called the middle-class. Therefore, the study of middle-class Baltimore women from the early- to mid-nineteenth century provides a most informative perspective on the lives of album quilters.

It is important when characterizing this group of nineteenth-century women to recognize that they were as individual 150 years ago as women are today. Some were paragons of tradition, some were progressives encouraging their fellow sex to push beyond the limited definitions of behavior, and of course many fell somewhere in between. It is possible, nevertheless, to describe a typical woman as the product of the time in which she lived.

Antebellum Baltimore women functioned within a very tightly defined set of standards for appropriate behavior. Probably no period previous to this point in American history so rigidly limited the role of women as did the middle decades of the nineteenth century. Virtue and selflessness were the key attributes, which every woman, but particularly middle and upper class women, strove to demonstrate in thought, word, and deed. These traits were vital to maintaining the values of the young republic as well as the religious and social morals of families at a time when technology was changing patterns of living rapidly.

Women had neither legal recourse nor the right to vote as a means of directing their lives, yet the majority accepted the role outlined for them, though not always without some struggle. They knew what society expected but found at times the required response more than they could deliver. Many women turned to religion for support when selflessness contrasted with their own inclinations, asking God to help them conform. And certainly other women knew that the life

Figure 57 "The Nest at Home," *Godey's Lady's Book*, February 1850.

society had shaped was unrealistic for them as individuals and, moreover, inequitable to their gender as a whole.

In order to understand these individuals, it is vital to understand the time in which they lived. A modern historian has characterized the nineteenth century as a period of unprecedented change. Politically, the country had relatively recently destroyed one set of loyalties in the Revolutionary War period and traded them for a new national allegiance. This new form of self-government was still considered an experimental one with no certainty of success. Physically, the country was expanding rapidly as wagon trains carried vast numbers of settlers west to populate the entire continent. And closely related to the growth of the country was the increase in population through immigration, which channeled diverse cultures and ethnic groups into both existing towns and new territories.[1]

During the eighteenth century, when most of the country operated primarily as an agrarian culture, the family worked as a single economic unit in which all members' functions overlapped. Industrialization resulted in changes for women by expanding their choices in some fields and reducing opportunities in others. For example, spinning, weaving, sewing, and food processing, all previously done in the home, were produced in factories. In addition, medicine, which earlier had been practiced by women, was taken over by men, while shopkeeping and innkeeping lost their old respectability.

As mid-Atlantic cities gained in wealth, living standards rose, and women became creatures of an increasingly fashionable and social world. Women's pursuits became ornamental, evidence that they could live leisured and economically unproductive lives. This new social pattern separated men's and women's spheres for the first time in America.[2]

Locally, these same forces, as well as others, altered the old order. In Maryland during the early-nineteenth-century, mineral wealth, shipping, canals, and rail enterprises bound the state's economy more to manufacturing, foreign exchange, and Ohio Valley farming

Figure 58 Singer sewing machine advertised in *Matchett's City Directory*, 1855-1856.

while decreasing the importance of cultivation of staple crops.³ Railroads boomed, and shipbuilding became the fourth largest source of employment in Baltimore by 1850.

The application of steam to myriad Baltimore industries resulted in new jobs for some while it displaced others. Steam technology transformed sugar refining, glass cutting, flour milling, plaster manufacturing, and spice grinding. Saw mills and textile mills were equally altered by the new source of power. Steam's even greater effect was to speed up transportation, accelerating the movement of people and materials by both rail and water.⁴ While people traveled between cities with unprecedented speed, and within the city more easily along the new omnibus routes, information could make the trip with the tap of a finger after Samuel Morse laid telegraph lines between Baltimore and Washington in 1843.

The character of the population in Baltimore underwent major changes in the middle years of the nineteenth century. Immigration, largely triggered by railroad and manufacturing opportunities, helped double the population in the thirty years from 1820 to 1850. Maryland's high proportion of immigrants distinguished it from the rest of the slave south where a homogeneous population helped maintain a white order based on black slavery. No such homogeneity existed in Maryland; the state had more foreign-born residents than any other East Coast slave state. Thirteen percent of Maryland whites had been born abroad, primarily in Germany, but also in Ireland, England, Scotland, and Wales. In fact, there were enough German-born Baltimore residents in 1850 to support three German-language newspapers.⁵

Poverty grew in Baltimore as the community expanded and became more foreign and as the economy shifted to an industrial one. New immigrants numbered eight thousand in 1832, and most of these recent arrivals, overwhelmingly young men, failed to find jobs. The economic slowdown of 1837, which lasted into the 1840s, made finding employment and keeping it "vicious."⁶

These economic and social alterations profoundly affected men's and women's lives. Men began building bridges, railroads, and all the infrastructure of cities, while establishing a new commercial culture based on wage earning. In the process, they turned away from the traditional religious and social values of humility and meekness which they had cherished but which were not conducive to forging an economic empire. Both men and women were aware of an upheaval in

Figure 59 Washing machine advertised in the *Baltimore American*, December 4, 1846.

their lives which required a balancing force. Men designated women to provide that stabilizing force and charged them with the obligation to uphold the values of the young republic and of society as well.

The "True Woman" was conceived to preserve family values within the home, which was her sphere, while men distinguished themselves in the public world of business and politics. The term "True Womanhood" was so widely used in magazines, gift books, novels, newspapers, and religious writing that it did not need to be defined. Every woman knew that she was judged by others, and indeed judged herself, on the basis of four qualities: purity, piety, submission, and domesticity. The *Young Ladies' Class Book*, published in Boston in 1831, advised that the "vestal flames of piety lighted up by Heaven in the breast of woman would throw its beams into the naughty world of men."⁷

These same messages were heard in Baltimore. In 1854, Virginia Wilson recorded hearing a lecture on taste and morals as well as a speech by Brantz Mayer on "The Women of the Nineteenth Century."⁸ Mayer lectured in New Orleans on the "True Mission of Women in Modern Society," and one assumes that he delivered the same restrictive message about family and home spheres to his Baltimore audience. Even the press played a role in shaping women's lives as a growing number of the population became literate. An article in the *Baltimore American and Daily Advertiser*, August 30, 1826, asked "Why is it that woman is more pious in her behavior and actions than the sex who arrogate to themselves the title of lord and master?" The writer concluded that the answer lay in the innate constitution of the female heart. The daily newspaper continued to advise women on the expectations society held for them. A year later, it listed twelve suggestions for wives, most of which were examples of submission, including "avoid contradicting your husband...," "never be curious to pry into your husband's concerns...," and "...leave him entirely master of his actions, to go and come whenever he thinks fit."[9]

German poet Johann Goethe was quoted on the subject of woman's sphere, defending men's efforts to limit the opportunities of women "to mere household duties, and to the government of the domestic circle." Goethe argued that by "entrusting to her the governance of his household," man placed her in "the highest and holiest position."[10]

The woman's sphere was restricted to the home and the family, where she not only upheld the religious and social values of the nation but was responsible for all domestic and child-care duties. A woman was expected to run her household in such a way that her husband would feel "pride and exultation in the possession of a companion who gives to his home charms that gratify every wish of his soul and render the haunts of dissipation hateful to him."[11] Moreover, she was to raise her daughters in her image, to be dutiful wives for their husbands, while she raised her sons to be patriots, moral men of steady habits, and successes in the public sphere. Clearly, a momentous burden fell to women.

The principles of "True Womanhood" were preached to women constantly, not only by men but also by their fellow women. Mrs. A. J. Graves set her readers straight regarding woman's role outside the home in 1842 when she wrote:

> Let man go forth into the world's arena, there achieve his triumphs, and with proud satisfaction receive his well-earned meed of fame; but what is there in fame to satisfy the heart of woman? Her social position forbids the love of glory and she stands not in need of it. It belongs to her to labor for good in her appropriate sphere for the sake of the good itself, seeking for no higher earthly reward than an approving conscience, and shrinking from applause as derogatory to the true dignity of her sex, and painful to her feelings as a woman.[12]

If fame and glory would not satisfy the heart of most nineteenth-century women, those qualities may have been just what a minority of their sisters sought. Although women were expected to find satisfaction in self-sacrifice and to serve the needs and interests of others, some women recognized that this was not the life for them. One woman confessed: "I think that to give happiness in married life a woman should possess oceans of self-sacrificing love and I, for one, haven't half of that self-forgetting spirit which I think is essential."[13] Some women pursued a vocation that could not be realized within the bonds of marriage. Several prominent Baltimoreans who made that choice include Anna Ella Carroll, military strategist and political propagandist; Sarah Miriam Peale, professional portrait painter; and Almira Hart Lincoln Phelps, scientist, educator and author. Of course, others who never achieved such prominence became the maiden aunts in many families.

Massachusetts-born astronomer Maria Mitchell phrased her opinion of the "True Woman" in mathematical terms: "A sphere is not made up of one but of a number of circles; women have diverse gifts, and to say that woman's sphere is the family circle is a mathematical absurdity."[14]

For a woman to speak out as Maria Mitchell did clearly threatened the social order. Mrs. A. J. Graves, reflecting the fear that women who stepped out of their proper place would cause social upheaval, wrote:

> When we find...even religious women forsaking home duties for public avocations, and hear an American moth-

Figure 60 Photograph of woman with "Ne Plus Ultra" sewing machine, c. 1855. Ross J. Kelbaugh Collection.

Figure 61 Photograph of a laundress, c. 1850. Ross J. Kelbaugh Collection.

er, with her infant in her arms, giving utterance to such complaints as these: "We cannot go to Congress; we cannot stand in the pulpit; we cannot be known; we must toil at home"; and when we know that this individual represents an increasing class, it is time for us to tremble for our homes.[15]

Certainly the "Cult of True Womanhood" was perhaps the greatest determinant of a woman's life in the early- to mid-nineteenth-century. The realities of health and hygiene also had a significant influence on the way women perceived their futures and responded to events in their lives. Medical science was strikingly unsophisticated one hundred fifty years ago. The germ theory of disease would not be recognized until the 1880s. No one really knew what caused disease or recognized the role played by rodents, mosquitoes, and flies in disease. This limited knowledge often made treatment of the sick questionable. One diarist noted that a friend was "quite downhearted at the prospect of a cancer in her breast. A lump has been there for some time, but of late her physician gives no encouragement to her of its being removed."[16] Other doctors employed ineffective and even counterproductive treatments such as "Sweedish [sic] leeches," which were widely advertised in newspapers from the period.

The prevalence of numerous fatal illnesses, some of which frequently recurred in epidemic proportions, poor hygiene, and ignorance about the causes of disease resulted in a terrific death rate among the young. All of these factors certainly compelled women to fear for the futures of their children and themselves, never knowing how long one would remain on this earth.

The Committee on Public Hygiene reported about 1850 on sanitation in Baltimore, noting filthy streets where animal and vegetable matter were regularly dumped by inhabitants: "This refuse, when not eaten by the swine, which are fortunately permitted to perambulate the streets at their pleasure, remain [sic] subject to the influences of decomposition." *The Sun* reported in September 1843, "A dead hog now lies exposed to the winds in Sharp Street, near Fayette. Remove it." Furthermore, there were no sewers or sewage treatment facilities, no comprehensive public water system, and no supervision of slaughterhouses. Pumps and public springs provided water to much of the population from potentially contaminated underground sources. The water's offensive taste and extreme hardness reportedly made it especially unpalatable. Smoke and fumes billowed from manufactories in every section of the city, even within a block or two of some of the finest residential neighborhoods. Glue, soap, gas, fertilizer, chemical, and white lead factories were scattered throughout the city.

As a result of these and other conditions, half of the population died before reaching the age of five years. In 1850, one quarter of the deaths in the city were of children under one year of age who died most often from cholera and scarlet fever. A child who lived to between five and ten years of age could well expect to live for an additional ten to fifteen years. The second largest proportion of deaths was of women in their twenties, thirties, and forties. Childbirth was only part of the explanation; ten times as many women died of consumption (i.e., tuberculosis) as died from childbirth. Mortality reports confirm how little was known about the causes of death--drinking cold water and teething were two causes of death reported every year.[17]

Letters and diaries of Baltimore women support the statistics reported by the health department. Hannah Mary Trimble wrote in 1850, "Heard of the death of Thomas Matthews' youngest child of scarlet fever, the third they have lost."[18] Matthews lost his three children in less than a week to this streptococcus bacteria. The same writer recorded the illness of a young woman friend, noting, "Consumption (that fatal destroyer of so many of America's fair daughters) had marked her for

Figure 62 Lutherville Female Seminary graduating class, 1859. Maryland Historical Society.

its own and she is rapidly passing away from this sunny earth."[19] As she watched her friends and relatives die from small pox, consumption, scarlet fever, cholera, a variety of fevers, and a great many unknown causes, sometimes after an illness of only a day or two, Hannah noted, "Life is indeed uncertain, the present moment only ours."[20] Certainly this sentiment reflected the prevailing attitude of women.

Motherhood presented a particular concern for both the expectant mother and her baby; childbirth was a significant risk to both. The Board of Health reported in 1849, "...we are struck with astonishment at the large number of children, who die during the process of parturition....We are free to admit that many, very many of these cases are beyond the reach of science, or the powers of medical skill."[21] Women were only too aware of these risks. One diarist noted as she awaited the birth of her first child, "Soon, if it is the will of God, I shall become a mother...but I would not indulge too much in fond anticipation, for I may myself be called at that time to die, to leave my babe, my beloved husband or the little one may just open its eyes to the light to close them forever."[22] It is significant that many women referred in their letters and diaries to childbirth as "sickness." The same author wrote four years later, "I must soon be laid upon a bed of sickness, and perhaps death!...In looking forward to my approaching confinement I cannot help feeling how uncertain is my life. Oh that I may be prepared for either life or death."[23]

Obstetrical wards of hospitals did not exist until the 1880s, so births took place at home attended by midwives or physicians. Yet this care was not necessarily adequate. Although the City had "possessed able and skilled teachers and practitioners of obstetrics" since the eighteenth century, for a variety of reasons, Baltimore's general practitioners were poorly trained in obstetrics. Midwives were not trained in any medical school setting and were essentially unsupervised, making them "in general, ignorant and inept in the art."[24]

Some of the deaths foisted upon the early-nineteenth-century population were the result not of disease, but of other forces equally beyond anyone's control. Newspapers reported fires, industrial accidents, and train crashes regularly and in vivid detail. Railroad accidents were so common and often caused the death of so large a number of passengers that the public "shuttered" to read the reports and called for greater controls on those "thoroughfares." Equally dreadful were the industrial accidents in which workers were severely injured or killed by the cogs of machinery or explosions of the steam engines running it.

Clearly, life was seen as a tenuous thing, which could be snatched away at any time. Partially because of this mentality of uncertainty and in part because churches proclaimed that religion had been given to women as a gift, piety along with church membership and regular church attendance were a significant part of women's lives. Religion or piety was perceived as the basis of a woman's virtue and the source of her strength. Indeed, every woman whose diary was read for this study reported not only both regular church attendance on Sunday and later in the week, but also frequent female prayer meetings at individual's homes. They also included written prayers in their diaries.

No doubt it was fortunate that society determined that God had given woman the gift of religion. Her faith clearly provided her the power to deal with the difficult times that life handed to her. When she was worried or anxious, a woman found that reading the Bible or stories of the lives of saints could put problems in a new perspective. More importantly, religion (or specifically church, Bible class, Sunday school attendance, and Sunday school teaching) neither distracted a woman from her proper sphere or feminine delicacy, nor made her less domestic or less submissive.

For much of the history of this country, women constituted the majority of church memberships, but by the nineteenth century, the cult of "True Womanhood" with its emphasis on piety, motherhood, and nurturing qualities swelled the female numbers far beyond earlier ratios. Voluntary church work fell to woman, who visited the sick and poor, distributed tracts, collected money for Bibles, raised funds to start missions both here and abroad, and taught Sunday school classes. In a small way, women felt that teaching Sunday school

Figure 63 "A Cold Water Party," *The Crystal Fount* by T.S. Arthur, 1850.

allowed them to influence the future of society. One president of the Baltimore McKendrean Female Sabbath School Society saw her job as "fitting the present generation to act their parts upon the great stage of human action."[25]

As testimony to the importance of religion, *The Sun* reported on May 23, 1843, "The ceremony of laying the corner stone of St. Peter's Church, at the corner of Poppleton and Hollins Streets, took place yesterday in the presence of about fifteen thousand people."[26] As that figure would have represented approximately fourteen percent of the city's population, it seems unlikely; however, the turnout must have been overwhelming.

Closely related to the religious fervor of the Second Great Awakening during the early-nineteenth century was the temperance movement. Begun in 1808 in Saratoga County, New York, with the organization of the first temperance society, the effort came to Maryland with the founding of the Maryland State Temperance Society in 1831. Though it was presumably men who overindulged and therefore needed to be persuaded to take the pledge against consuming ardent spirits, much of the proselytizing came from women. The movement provided them a public role in shaping society. At the first anniversary meeting of the Maryland State Temperance Society, a speaker prevailed upon the

> fair Daughters of the land ...[for] assistance in promoting the cause of Temperance. On you especially devolves the pleasing, anxious task....Say then shall not this power be exerted, at least within your domestic circles, (and why not everywhere?) to expose the evils and to stay the ravages of the hateful vice which no force of language can too strongly denounce?[27]

Temperance was a clear case of the need for women to "throw their beams into the naughty world of men." Gift books, marketed for women and containing moralistic writing, always included a variety of essays, poems, and short stories on temperance. Published pamphlets and books advocated cold water parties where no alcoholic beverages would be served. It was certainly in the best interests of women to speak out against the evils of alcohol consumption. Drinking had the potential to ruin not only the reputation and credit of a man but his ability to support his family. Temperance societies exacted a pledge from their members not to drink intoxicating beverages as well as a small weekly dues, which provided benefits to the widows of their former members. The printed by-laws and rosters of these organizations list large memberships in the 1830s and 1840s.

Abolition was another reform movement in which some women became involved. Closely related to the Sunday School movement and probably encouraged by churches, it allowed women to work for the liberty of a group of people while they themselves remained confined within their own domestic sphere. There is very little evidence of Baltimore women's participation in abolition. A single mention of the cause occurred in a diary where the writer mentioned attending a lecture on the free soil question. She did not say where she stood on this issue, which opposed the extension of slavery into the new territory acquired from Mexico in 1848.

The women's rights movement formally began with the Seneca Falls Convention in New York in 1848, called to address inequalities in education, employment opportunities, and legal rights. Participants in the movement felt that purity, piety, domesticity, and submission were inadequate qualities by which to define a woman. Certainly there were extreme inequalities in education.

Hannah More, a British poet and novelist, championed higher education for women but was careful to restrict its purpose to preparing a young girl for life as a wife and mother or the mistress of a family. Early in the century, women's schools were not much more than finishing schools, teaching young ladies how to be older ladies who could attract a good husband and enhance his home. Needlework was taught as a sign of gentility, not simply as a necessary craft. Painting and other fine arts were part of the curriculum. By the third decade of the nineteenth century, some strides in women's education had occurred. Course offerings included academic subjects such as chemistry, composition, history, mathematics, grammar and geography.

Godey's Lady's Book joined the discussion on the merits of teaching women mathematics and the sciences. In 1839, an essay entitled "Learning vs. Housewifery" argued for teaching women more than domestic arts and old-fashioned accomplishments. Chemistry could help the woman "who superintends the roasting of a leg of mutton" if she understands the "action of the free caloric!" Geometry could enable her to cut out a garment more skillfully, while astronomy could "give some tolerable hints to the formation of a bed quilt." Phrenology was "absolutely necessary.... Every mother should be able to make a scientific examination of her own children's craniums, whereby she may discover the peculiar bent of their genius."[28]

Although Godey's logic seemed flawed, it could be argued that a woman's education might enable her to be a more effective mother. To clarify the importance of the mother in her child's education, Edward A. M'Nally wrote in 1819, "If a child have a negligent, ignorant father, but an enlightened mother, he is still safe, but if he have an ignorant, imprudent mother, be the father ever so well informed, he is in danger of being cut off for ever from the paths of rectitude and esteem, if continued under her management."[29]

By the middle of the nineteenth century, Baltimore offered twenty-two public female primary schools, eleven female grammar schools and three female high schools. There were also a number of private institutes, which Baltimore girls attended. Each September, the newspapers announced the start of a number of small academies operated by two or three instructors. Boarding schools opened their doors throughout the state in the 1830s. Catholic boarding schools, including St. Joseph's Academy in Emmittsburg, the Academy of the Visitation in Georgetown, and Notre Dame in Baltimore, were well-known for providing quality educations to young women regardless of their religious affiliation. Other institutions included Hannah More Academy, 1834; Ingleside Academy, near Catonsville, 1845; and a number of Quaker schools. Many female seminaries were run by a male board of trustees who perpetuated the restrictive definition of the woman's sphere.

More advanced education for women was not available until the middle of the century. The Baltimore Female College, incorporated in 1849, offered the first higher education in the city, followed by the Mt. Washington Female College, which a Lutheran group founded in 1856. These colleges offered limited courses, far inferior to a men's college curriculum, consisting principally of teacher's training. This was nevertheless a first response to the realization that not all women married and those who did not needed a profession, which would occupy their time and provide a means of support, respectability, and usefulness.

For all married women or others who kept households, regardless of the amount of household help available to them, domestic activities could easily occupy nearly all of their day. Countless books told housewives how to organize their households. One Philadelphia author instructed her readers that a woman of good sense:

> must begin the day with an early breakfast, requiring each person to be in readiness to take their seats when the muffins, buckwheat cakes, etc. are placed on the table. This looks social and comfortable. When the family breakfast by detachments, the table remains a tedious time; the servants are kept from their morning meal and a complete derangement takes place in the whole business of the day.[30]

The Improved Housewife published in 1846, in addition to providing regular recipes and cookery for the sick, instructed a woman in such things as how to extract the rancidity of butter; how to preserve cream for steamboat or sea voyages; how to keep eggs for Christmas; how to wash woolens or calicoes; how to clean bedsteads, carpets and blankets; how to keep rats out of the food stored in the cellar (if they are a problem); and how to dye fabric or yarn various colors, along with hundreds of other useful bits of advice.

The diaries of women reveal that sewing, food shopping and preparation, food preserving, laundry, housecleaning, and caring for the sick filled the majority of their day. Regardless of how much housework was relegated to servants or slaves, one constant chore in every woman's life was sewing. In virtually every household, rich or poor, women sewed nearly every day. Even those women who had their dresses made by a dressmaker mended, made servants' clothing, made children's clothes and men's shirts, and constructed their own lingerie and "home dresses." And every stitch was done by hand as sewing machines, first advertised about 1854, were marketed to professional seamstresses and not widely available until after the Civil War.

Domestic chores filled needs of which twentieth-century women have no concept. Preserving dozens of pineapples, apricots, berries, and other fruit; making gallons of catsup; sorting coffee and hulling beans; clear starching; and doing the fancy German wash were all mentioned by diarists. One forty-three-year-old woman admitted that the responsibilities of a household overwhelmed her:

> If 'twere not that other's comfort more than mine was to be considered I should plead strongly for respite—'Tis a long wearisome time since I first entered upon the duties involved in domestic life and with no aid save that of ordinary hirelings I have entertained much company, nursed in considerable sickness, besides catering to the taste and appetites of many. I have stumbled along day by day and year by year until I have fairly broken down. Give thy support oh Father to continue to fulfill each duty as it arises...Retired weary as usual.[31]

Although women worked long and hard to maintain their households, they certainly found time for entertainment and pleasure. Diaries record a variety of diversions beyond the predictable entertaining and visiting with friends and other family members. When traveling away from home, women seemed awed by nature where waterfalls, rocky cliffs or rivers might have been described as "sublime." They returned with souvenirs of leaves and flowers taken from a particularly appealing spot on their trip and pasted the mementos in scrapbooks. Factories and other industrial sites also attracted visitors. Diaries recorded impressions of large manufacturing plants, which were a novelty during the first decades of the nineteenth century.

In town, there was a selection of entertainments. A lecture by William Thackeray or others, school and college graduations, numerous theatre and concert performances, church fairs, boat and railroad excursions, husking and quilting parties, visits to the new park-like Green Mount Cemetery, gardening, benefits, and curiosity and art exhibits provided diversions.

The recession of 1837, the huge influx of immigrants, and the displacement of workers as a result of new technology certainly created the climate in which women's charity could flourish. Women participated in benevolent organizations, founding them, serving as officers, or contributing time and effort to their causes. A variety of associations for children, the aged, and the poor met the needs of underprivileged citizens while they provided women with another outlet for involvement outside the home.

Although the economic climate provided ample cause, an equally powerful influence on the formation of women's groups must have been a reaction to the nearly total absence of women's legal status. At marriage, a woman's existence was merged with that of her husband, and she lost all legal rights to property previously deeded to her, to her wages, to her own inheritance, to will her property as she chose, to sue, or to enter into a contract. No woman had the right to vote or hold elective office where she could alter these laws, nor could she serve on a jury. Even divorce laws were discriminatory. In the eyes of the law, a married woman was grouped with infants, idiots, and lunatics.

Many women questioned the restrictive boundaries of their sphere. Susan B. Anthony, the Grimke sisters, and Elizabeth Cady Stanton were prominent reformers, but countless unknown women also strove to expand the dimensions of their influence. Nevertheless, these efforts caused considerable anxiety about the impact of increased women's rights on the family and society.

Women in the early- to mid-nineteenth century endured physical and emotional stresses far beyond those generally recognized now. The prevailing view of this period, that it was a time of genteel and gracious social behavior when life was slower and less complicated than today's, seems to distort the actual experience. Women's writing reveals that the pressures to conform to society's clearly dictated concepts of a "True Woman," the incessant physical and emotional challenges of keeping house and raising a family, the adversities of disease, and threat of early death seemed so severe and relentless at times as to be nearly insupportable.

NOTES

1 Keith E. Melder, *Beginnings of Sisterhood, The American Woman's Rights Movement, 1800 to 1850*, 1-2.

2 Ibid., 6.

3 Robert J. Brugger, *Maryland: A Middle Temperament, 1634-1980*, 177.

4 Ibid., 216.

5 Ibid., 255.

6 Ibid., 232.

7 Ibid., 152.

8 Wilson Papers, Manuscripts Division, Maryland Historical Society, MS. 833, 1854.

9 *Baltimore American and Commercial Daily Advertiser*, November 28, 1827.

10 "The Sphere of Woman." Translated from the German of Goethe. *Godey's Magazine and Lady's Book*, March, 1850, XIII. 209.

11 Mrs. Mary Randolph, *The Virginia Housewife or Methodical Cook*, XIII.

12 Mrs. A.J. Graves, *Woman in America, Being an Examination into the Moral and Intellectual Condition of American Female Society*, 202.

13 Lee Virginia Chambers-Shiller, *Liberty a Better Husband: Single Women in America: the Generations of 1780-1840*, 5.

14 Ibid., 62.

15 Graves, 58.

16 Diary of Mary Matthews Dobbin, Manuscripts Division, Maryland Historical Society, MS. 2385, June 22, 1853.

17 James Wynne, M.D., *Extract from the First Report of the Committee on*

Public Hygiene of the American Medical Association, Sanitary Report of Baltimore. 1850, 231.

18 Diary of Hannah Mary Trimble, Manuscripts Division, Maryland Historical Society, MS. 2517, February 1, 1850.

19 Ibid., January 7, 1850.

20 Ibid., April 18, 1850.

21 John F. Monmonier, M.D., J.F.C. Hadel and Edward J. Chaisty, M.D., *Report of the Board of Health*.

22 Wilson, 1851.

23 Wilson, 1855.

24 William Travis Howard, Jr., M.D., *Public Health Administration and the Natural History of Disease in Baltimore*, Maryland *1797-1920*, 439.

25 Anne M. Boylan, *Sunday School, The Formation of an American Institution, 1790-1880*, 117.

26 *The Sun*, May 23, 1843.

27 J.C. Herbert, "An Address Delivered at the First Anniversary Meeting of the Maryland State Temperance Society, Annapolis," January 5, 1832.

28 *Godey's Lady's Book and Ladies American Magazine*, August, 1839, 95.

29 Edward A. McNally, *The Importance of Education particularly to Females…(Baltimore, 1819)*, 49.

30 Mrs. Mary Randolph, *The Virginia Housewife or Methodical Cook*, XI.

31 Diary of Mary Matthews Dobbin, Manuscripts Division, Maryland Historical Society, MS. 2385, September 4, 1853.

CATALOGUE SECTION

Relevant dates and locations have been provided for individual quilters wherever they are known. Despite the many names recorded on Baltimore album quilts, it is very difficult to learn about specific women in the mid-nineteenth century unless the names of fathers and/or husbands are known. Popular names were quite limited and, in many cases, several women with the same name and of the appropriate ages were found; in most instances, we could not determine which one should be associated with a specific quilt. Occasionally, family, neighborhood, or church groupings represented on a quilt helped determine to which women the names referred.

The sense of anonymity of mid-nineteenth century middle-class women is reinforced by the fact that we have no pictures of the women whose names appear on the Baltimore album quilts in the Maryland Historical Society collection. These women were not of the status to have patronized portrait painters; and, although a daguerreotype studio had been established in Baltimore as early as 1840, photography was still experimental, expensive, and little-used at the time these quilts were made. In fact, the name on a quilt square seems to be the only surviving evidence that many of these people ever existed.

Please note that most of these quilts were given to the Maryland Historical Society by descendants of their original owners lending credence to the family stories which accompany them.

The measurements of the quilts are approximations which may vary slightly depending on the exact part of the quilt being measured; length is given before width. The number of quilting stitches recorded is the average number visible on the top of the quilt within a one-inch space.

Specific quilt squares are designated according to the convention of assigning a letter of the alphabet to vertical rows starting with A on the left side of the quilt and assigning a number to the horizontal rows starting with 1 at the top of the quilt; thus, the uppermost left square is referred to as square A1.

Catalogue 1
Maryland Red-and-Green Appliqué Quilt
c. 1850

Made by Elizabeth Ann Rogers (1830-1862), daughter of William S. Rogers and wife of Joshua Lynch.

Plain and printed cotton; quilting 16 stitches to the inch.

Square size approximately 13 1/2 x 14 inches; quilt size approximately 98 1/4 x 102 1/4 inches.

Gift of Mrs. William C. Kirwan (daughter of Elizabeth Rogers Lynch), 52.19.2

    Appliquéd quilts with repetitive squares developed during the 1840s in the mid-Atlantic region. This quilt capitalizes on the vibrant Turkey-red dyed and the green-figured cottons, which became widely available and less expensive about 1840. Also by that time, strong, cheap, factory-spun sewing thread was more easily acquired and encouraged abundant quilting. Symmetrical, four-part, red-and-green designs like this also were used for individual squares on Baltimore album quilts where they were often placed in the corners (see Catalogue 4, 15, 23, 24, 28, and 31). The sawtooth border design was used for a number of early Baltimore album quilts (see Catalogue 14).

Catalogue 2
Maryland Red-and-Green Appliquéd Quilt
c. 1845-1855

Made by Mary Dove Travers (1777-1857) of Dorchester County, Maryland.

Plain and printed cottons; quilting 9 stitches to the inch.

Square size approximately 15 1/4 x 15 1/4 inches; quilt size approximately 97 1/4 x 98 1/4 inches.

Gift of George M. Radcliffe (great-great-grandson of Mary Travers), 92.35

    Family tradition indicates that Mary Travers made many quilts, a number of which are treasured by her descendants. Although typical of the red-and-green style, this quilt hints at the more naturalistic developments of the Baltimore album quilt style. The little leafy sprigs at each corner of the red, crossed fleur-de-lis designs are very realistic, and the classically-inspired swag-and-tassel border would become a favorite frame for Baltimore album quilts (see Catalogue 5, 10, 23 for related examples).

51

Catalogue 3
Maryland Chintz-Appliquéd and Pieced Quilt
c. 1835

Made by Catherine Mitchell (1775-1847) at Mitchell's Garden on the Choptank River. Descended from the maker to a niece, then to her niece, Elizabeth Frazier Benson, mother of the donor.

Chintz, plain and printed cottons; quilting 10 stitches to the inch.

Center square size approximately 37 1/4 x 37 3/4 inches; quilt size approximately 103 1/2 x 104 inches.

Gift of Mrs. William Humes Houston, 50.56.1

    Chintz-appliquéd quilts with a central medallion were an English style of decorative bedcoverings, which were especially popular in the southern United States during the first half of the nineteenth century. This manner of needlework, later called *broderie perse*, made the most of a small amount of expensive, usually imported chintz. The pieced central square was a feature of a number of Maryland quilts made during the first half of the nineteenth century. The placing of chintz elements in regular, repetitive areas of this quilt introduces the concept of measured squares, which became characteristic of Baltimore album quilts.
    The giraffe in the border chintz is a wonderful example of the whimsical nature of English chinoiserie chintzes. This fabric has been reproduced recently by an English decorating firm at a cost of approximately $100 per yard; the original would probably have been at least the equivalent value when this elegant quilt was made. The exotic animals such as lions, tigers, elephants, monkeys, and parrots that appear on Baltimore album quilts may have been copied from the designs on chintz fabrics.

Catalogue 4
Maryland Chintz-Appliquéd Bedcovering
c. 1840

According to family history, this quilt was made by a midwife for Ella Calvert who was born at "Riversdale" in 1841; while the date appears accurate, the elegant character and style of this quilt make it more likely to have been made by or for Ella's mother, Charlotte Augusta Norris who married Charles Benedict Calvert in 1839. It is possible that the midwife quiltmaker was a slave or African-American servant.

Chintz, plain and printed cottons; quilting 15 stitches to the inch.

Center square size approximately 62 1/2 x 64 inches; other squares size approximately 15 1/2 x 15 1/2 inches; quilt size approximately 115 1/2 x 116 inches.

Gift of Mrs. William Ellicott, 45.14.1

    Chintz-appliquéd quilts encouraged needlewomen to exercise their own artistry by creating individualistic floral compositions. Such quilts may also have inspired the local Baltimore elaborations of cut, layered, padded, and embroidered appliqué as methods of imitating the gorgeously naturalistic patterns on expensive chintzes. The chintz borders of quilts like this probably influenced the appliquéd vine and floral swag borders of some Baltimore album quilts (see Catalogue 7, 14, and 21 for examples). This quilt provides a stylistic transition joining the English chintz-appliquéd medallion quilt type with the German-American red-and-green appliquéd square type. It is only a small step from this to the classic Baltimore album quilt. On this example, the appliqué work was actually done on a woven Marseilles-type fabric, a feature found on a few other fine Maryland chintz-appliquéd bedcoverings.

Catalogue 5
Maryland Chintz-Appliquéd Quilt
c. 1840

Made by Ann B. Cator of Taylor's Island, Dorchester County, Maryland.

Chintz, plain and printed cottons; quilting 8-9 stitches to the inch.

Center square size approximately 41 x 40 3/4 inches; quilt size approximately 99 x 101 inches.

Gift of Mrs. Harry Morrison (great-granddaughter of maker), 53.128.1

By confining the central design within a strict square placed "on point" and using an appliquéd swag border, the maker of this quilt was moving towards the album quilt format of collected appliquéd calico squares. This format came directly from ceremonial cloths called *rumal* from northern India, which presented a central, flower-filled square on point (oriented on the diagonal) surrounded by numerous borders with squares in each corner of the cloth.*

The central bird was cut from chintz yardage, which also shows up on other early American chintz-appliqué quilts. A New York City quilt with the same falcon or hawk-like bird, now at The Metropolitan Museum of Art, is dated about 1803.** A strikingly similar quilt including this same bird appliquéd in a center square on point surrounded by *broderie perse* sprigs and a series of chintz and appliquéd calico borders was given to the Birmingham Museum of Art by Mrs. William James Hagan III in memory of Louise Warten Hagan, William James Hagan Jr., and William James Hagan III. That quilt is thought to have been made by Martha Hobbs Lucas in Athens, Alabama, at the very beginning of the nineteenth century.***

The colorful birds introduce a motif, which appears regularly on Baltimore album quilts. The appliquéd-chintz sprigs appear as the designs on some quilt squares in early Baltimore album quilts (see Catalogue 25). The arrangement of this quilt is similar to that of Catalogue 22 and the quilted pinwheels in the border here are similar to the appliquéd ones on that quilt. The sawtooth inner border design and the appliquéd swag border appear on a number of early Baltimore album quilts.

* see Phillips, Barty. *Fabrics and Wallpapers: Sources Design and Inspiration*, 147.
** see Peck, Amelia. *American Quilts and Coverlets in The Metropolitan Museum of Art*, 16-19.
*** see Adams, E. Bryding. "Variations in Quilts," *Antiques and The Arts Weekly*, November 13, 1993, 106.

Catalogue 6
Maryland Chintz-Appliquéd Album Quilt
c. 1840

Believed to have been designed by Mrs. Francis Montague Montell (neé Joanna Penelope Elizabeth Cushing) for Sarah Anne Bartow who married Mrs. Montell's son Francis T. Montell.

Chintz, printed striped cotton, plain muslin; inking; quilting 14 stitches to the inch.

Square size approximately 13 x 13 inches; quilt size approximately 103 x 89 1/4 inches.

Gift of Mrs. Mary Bartow Steuart (granddaughter of Mrs. F. T. Montell), 55.8.1

It is somewhat unusual to find a chintz-appliquéd quilt composed of squares rather than a bordered central medallion. This is a true album quilt because each square bears an inscription naming a close friend or female member of Joanna Cushing Montell's family. This is a transitional quilt combining elements of *broderie perse* and conventional appliqué on the way to the Baltimore album quilt style. The open floral wreaths in several squares on this quilt are similar enough to layered appliqué ones on Baltimore album quilts to have served as models (see Catalogue 7). The inscribed names include:

Aunt Annie (square B2)
Mother (squares A3, A7, C1, C9, G9, I3, I7)
Aunt Tilly (square H8)
Elizabeth B... (square E5)
Martha Bartow (square E3)
Adelaide N. Blair (square H4)
Miss H. Blair (square F6)
Mathilda H. Blair (square C3)
Emma (squares A1, B4, B6, D2, E7, F2, G1, G7)
Aunt Madgie (square B8)
Eliza Montell (square I9), born 1790, living at 84 Pratt Street, Baltimore
Fanny Montell (square C7), probably living at 84 Pratt Street, Baltimore
Frank M. Montell (square D4)
Grandma Montell (squares A5, C5, E1, E9. I5)
John B. Montell (squares F4, G3)
Sarah W. Montell (square G5)
M. E. Montell (square I9)
Mrs. ? Sterling (squares A9, D8, I1)
Betty Wh?t?mes (square D6)
Adal? Wildgoss (square F8)
Eliza Wildgoss (square H2)
Emily Wildgoss (square F4), born 1827, living at 84 Pratt Street, Baltimore
Mary Wildgoss (square H6)

Catalogue 7
Baltimore Album Quilt
1852

Designs attributed to Mary Simon; possibly made by relatives and friends of Laura Horton at the time of her marriage to Zedekiah Tarman. Or, possibly made for Mary Heiner by women of the First Reformed Church.

Plain and printed cottons, chintz, silk; inking; quilting 18 stitches to the inch.

Square size approximately 18 1/4 x 16 1/2 inches; quilt size approximately 107 x 105 inches.

The Middendorf Fund purchase, 91.17

This exquisite quilt ranks among the finest dozen Baltimore album quilts known and is thought to represent the work of the best-known and most easily recognized master designer, Mary Simon (see p. 16). Few Baltimore album quilts combine such beautiful and well-coordinated designs, so many unusual fabrics, such a large number of poignant inscriptions, and such close, ornamental quilting. The carefully composed floral squares may be judged as works of fine rather than folk art.

This is one of the few quilts that may have been a wedding quilt; most squares include the name of a female member of Laura Horton's family and a Biblical quotation, primarily from the last chapter of the Book of Proverbs, which describes a virtuous woman. Sadly, the bride died within a year or so of her marriage, and the quilt is believed to have been inherited by her sister or young niece and passed down through that family in Frederick, Maryland. A recently discovered 1888 Horton family letter, which may refer to this quilt, talks about a quilt made by women of the First Reformed Church and presented to their pastor's wife, Mary Heiner. That quilt was eventually given to Elizabeth Parrish Slick, daughter of Catherine Horton Parrish; Catherine was the niece of Laura Horton Tarman. The inscribed names include:

Mrs. Kate C. Baugher (square E3)

Anna M. Boyer (square C2), born 1820; her father Jacob Boyer was a partner in Boyer & Diffenderffer, grocer and iron merchants, 1840-1841. She married James Hamilton March 15, 1853, and lived at Albemarle and Pratt Streets, Baltimore.

Mary Catherine Davis (square A1), died 1864

Julia A. Decker (square D1), born 1805, married to Jacob F. Decker, a clerk; they lived at 135 Fayette Street, Baltimore.

Mrs. Susan Decker (square A3), born 1775, married to George Decker, lived at 1 South High Street, Baltimore.

Lizzie Diffenderffer (square C5); either the Elizabeth Diffenderffer who lived 1786-1866 and is buried at Green Mount Cemetery; or the Elizabeth Diffenderffer who was confirmed in 1803 at the age of fifteen.

Sarah A. (Ann) Diffenderffer (square C3), born 1815, maiden name Todd, married to John A. Diffenderffer, merchant, lived at 39 Baltimore Street, Baltimore; belonged to a Methodist Church.

Lizzie Duhurst (square A4), born 1825, lived at 32 North Gay Street, Baltimore; member of the First German Reformed Church.

Frances A. Finlay (square B1), born 1829, married Dr. William L. Willis May 5, 1853, lived at 97 Hanover Street, Baltimore; member of the First German Reformed Church.

Charlotte Heiner (square C1), born 1812, married Thomas Rudisell February 9, 1860, lived at 81 East Pratt Street, Baltimore; member of the First German Reformed Church.

Elizabeth Horton (square E1), confirmed in the First German Reformed Church, April 13, 1838.

Laura H. Horton (square D2), 1825-1853, married Zedekiah Tarman October 19, 1852. In 1850, lived at 61 Sharp Street, Baltimore, where Eliza Maynard (see below) also lived; joined the First German Reformed Church in 1847.

Ellen Keller (square D4)

Evelyn Mason (square C4)

Eliza M. Maynard (square D2), born 1820, lived at 61 Sharp Street, Baltimore; married to Robert F. Maynard, merchant.

Gertrude Monteiro (Square A5), belonged to First German Reformed Church.

Susan Frances Porter (square E5), 1832-1911, married Dr. Jacob Weaver Houck November 1852; belonged to First German Reformed Church and known to have been very involved in charitable work.

Christianna Selback (square B4)

Margaret A. Smith (square D5)

Mary A. Smith (square D3)

Amanda Troxell (square E4), born 1832; lived in Emmitsburg, Maryland.

Mary Ann Vansant (square E2), died 1877; married to Joshua Vansant who owned a hat shop and became a mayor of Baltimore; lived at 115 Baltimore Street, Baltimore; confirmed in the First German Reformed Church May 8, 1848.

Mrs. Jacob Yeisley (square B2), maiden name Springer; married Jacob Yeisley, a carpenter, and lived at 121 Gough Street, Baltimore.

Mrs. Zimmerman (square B3)

Catalogue 8
Baltimore Album Quilt Top
1852

Designs attributed to Mary Simon; believed to have been made for a Capt. Aust.

Plain and printed cottons, silk, velvet, brocade; inking; no quilting.

Square size approximately 19 1/4 x 19 inches; quilt top size approximately 93 1/8 x 77 inches.

Gift of Mrs. Frances Marie Smart, Mrs. James Whitaker, Mrs. Joseph F. Wood, 79.29.1

A number of unquilted tops in the Baltimore album style survive; in most such cases, it is not known whether they simply never were finished or were meant to be bedspreads. This quilt top is fondly called "Little Lucy" after the girl in the lower left corner who is thought to be a character from a children's book. The butcher in the upper right corner is especially lifelike and amusing; perhaps this square represents the occupation of a family friend or relative. The ship in the lower right corner probably refers to Captain Aust for whom the quilt top is said to have been made. The upper left square with a plow, farm implements, and bunches of root vegetables is the emblem of an agricultural society. Inscribed names include:

Celest C. Barrenger (square D2), born 1837; lived at 26 Lewis Street, Baltimore.

Mary E. Barringer (square C1), born 1833; lived at 26 Lewis Street, Baltimore; deaf and dumb.

Sarah E. Bombarger (square A4)

Andrew Brunner (square B2), born 1805; married to Elizabeth Ann Brunner in 1826; lived at 54 Pearl Street where he was a "segar factor/tobacconist."

William T. Buckhold

Barbara Dames (square D5), born 1834 and lived in Baltimore County.

Diana Dames (square D4), born 1786; married to Augustus Dames, a gardner; lived in Baltimore County.

John Dames (square A2), born 1826, a gardner in Baltimore County.

Mary Dames (square D1)

William Dames (square A1), born 1811, married to Alice Dames; was a gardner in Baltimore County.

Amanda Su Gelbach (square B1), born 1836, of Baltimore County.

Miss Mary E. Lambert (square B3), born 1831, lived at 197 North Exeter Street, Baltimore.

Mrs. Rosina Lambert (square D3), born 1807; married to Cornelius W. Lambert, a constable; lived at 197 North Exeter Street, Baltimore.

John McCullogh (square C4)

Cynthia Scofield (square B5)

Henry Scofield (square B4)

Solomon Scofield (square C3)

Fanny Walker (square A5), maiden name Smith, married to Samuel Walker October 25, 1792, a dry goods merchant; belonged to a Presbyterian Church.

Rosanna Walker (square A3), born 1824.

Catalogue 9
Baltimore Album Quilt Top
1849

Believed to have been made for Thomas Lewis Darnall at the time of his marriage to Adeline Virginia Bartroff.

Plain and printed cottons; cotton embroidery and inking; no quilting.

Center square size approximately 17 1/2 x 17 1/4 inches; small square size approximately 8 3/4 x 8 1/2 inches; quilt top size approximately 78 1/4 x 78 1/4 inches.

Gift of Douglas L. Darnall (grandson of T. L. Darnall), 57.80.2

The central basket square appears to have been designed by the most proficient, Baltimore album quilt designer, Mary Simon (see p. 16). But, the style of the unusually small surrounding blocks is atypical and resembles those on a recently discovered 1842-1843 Baltimore album quilt. One or a few fine Mary Simon-type squares are often found focused in the central area of a Baltimore album quilt with other, more individualistic squares in the surrounding area. The following people who are named on the quilt lived in Montgomery County, Maryland; the friendship verses accompanying many of the names are particularly poignant:

SAF (square A3)
L. A. Dawson July 14th '49 (square B2)
  In after years when thou perchance
  As thoughts of Auld Lang Syne arise
  Midst other scenes should cast a glance
  Along these squares should thine eyes
  Rest on this tribute, Think of me
  Think kindly—as I shall of Thee.
L. E. Dawson July 24th (square C7)
  May friendship open unto you
  The paths of peace and holy love
  May lifes continual joys renew
  May hope not to deception prove
  May sweet contentment round you ? th?
  Such bliss as may be found.
Hester W. V?? M.. Augt 22 1849 (square E1)
  May God continue still to bless
  My friend with lasting happiness
  May every day add such delights
  And bliss ? ? each night.
Sarah A. E. W... Friendship (square E7)
Mrs. Elizabeth Darnall Montgomery Co. Maryland Augt 8th 1849 (square F2),
  1801-1885, maiden name Young, married a farmer, Fieldes Darnall in 1824.
Elizabeth Isabel King August 1849 (square G3)
H. A. Piles (square G5) for Hulday A. Pile(s),
  1830-1910, married Richard G. White January 1853
Mrs. L. Dawson Montgomery Co. Maryland Aug 1849
  Friendship's Gift (square G7)

Catalogue 10
Baltimore Album Quilt
c. 1850

Plain and printed cottons, velvet; silk and wool embroidery; inking; quilting 10 stitches to the inch.

Square size approximately 16 3/4 x 16 3/4 inches; quilt size approximately 104 3/4 x 106 inches.

Gift of Mrs. Alan D. Chesney, 66.79.1

    The history of this delightful quilt is unknown but the design of the man and woman holding hands in the second row may indicate a wedding or anniversary. The squares go together very well but probably represent the work of several designers executed by a number of talented hands. The four most elaborate squares—man and woman, Baltimore's Washington Monument, man with a flag, and the bold eagle square—are attributed to Mary Simon. The four squares placed between them may be an alternative, more stylized phase of her work. The rose wreath in the bottom row may be a Designer II square; in addition, there are a number of especially clever individual squares and cut-paper designs forming a catalogue of Baltimore album quilt square types. The figure with the flag is intriguing; he may be a sailor with the naval flag of the independent Republic of Texas, or he may be a soldier in one of numerous Mexican War period uniforms with a United States flag. Understandably, many quiltmakers found it impossible to execute the proper number of five-point stars in miniature and merely indicated the general form of the national flag.

67

Catalogue 11
Baltimore Album Quilt
1849

Believed to have been made by Amanda (Alexander) Porter during the first year of her marriage to William Porter, a Baltimore mariner; they were married February 1, 1848, and lived at 87 Montgomery Street. Amanda is believed to have been born about 1830 and William in 1822.

Chintz, plain and printed cotton; silk embroidery and inking; quilting 7-8 stitches to the inch.

Square size approximately 17 x 16 inches; quilt size approximately 88 x 105 3/8 inches.

Gift of Mrs. S. A. Stuart (granddaughter of Amanda and William Porter), 51.94.1

This quilt exemplifies the charm of Baltimore album quilts. Among the more interesting squares are the central design of the Holy Bible and dove of peace, the temperance fountain square in the bottom row, the ship—perhaps deliberately indicating Mr. Porter's occupation as a sailor, a patriotic eagle square, and a *compotier* of fruit closely resembling theorem paintings on velvet, which had been popular genteel pursuits during the 1830s. It is possible that the most elaborate squares represent the early design work of Mary Simon before she perfected her more ostentatious and intricately layered appliqué style. Several squares employ surprisingly large prints including designs that appear to have been cut from bandannas.

The plain cotton backing carries the stamp of a Baltimore County bleachyard, the Providence D., B. & C. Company. The chintz border and cross-stitched date *April the 3 A.D. 1849* and inscription *Amanda M. Porter/William Porter* are characteristics of pre-1850 Baltimore album quilts.

Catalogue 12
Baltimore Album Quilt
c. 1850

Plain and printed cottons; quilting 10 stitches to the inch.

Square size approximately 16 1/2 x 16 1/2 inches; quilt size approximately 104 1/2 x 104 inches.

Gift of Mrs. Eleanor J. Tyler, 60.19.1

    This quilt presents a particularly broad range of skill levels; the central, elaborate basket design is attributed to Mary Simon (see p. 16) while the square in the upper left corner is as simple as any found on Baltimore album quilts. The border, although a little stiff, required considerable appliqué skill. The leaf-and-berry-heart square below the basket is a design that is found on a number of other Baltimore album quilts (for example, Catalogue 27, 32), but several of the other squares and the holly-and-leaf border are individualistic. This quilt truly appears to be a collection or "album" of different appliqué designs executed in a wide variety of the fabrics available in Baltimore.

Catalogue 13
Baltimore Album Quilt
c. 1845-1850

Inscribed Elizabeth McComas, Mary A. McComas, and Mary E. Dorsey

Plain cottons; quilting 11-12 stitches to the inch.

Square size approximately 17 x 16 3/4 inches; quilt size approximately 113 1/2 x 115 inches.

Gift of Mrs. Anne E. Bannon, 66.59.1

This quilt is thought to be quite early by virtue of the red sawtooth borders on the appliquéd squares and the prevalence of geometric patterns. The two reverse-appliquéd red princess-feather squares are handsome examples of this demanding technique, which appears on some Baltimore album quilts. Although the designs are less visually complex than those on many Baltimore album quilts, they represent technically difficult needlework. Census records for 1850 list several women by each of the names on this quilt: a Mary McComas, wife of a gunsmith in Baltimore; a Mary McComas, wife of a farmer in Harford County (birthplace of the Baltimore gunsmith); Elizabeth McComas, age 50 of Harford County; Elizabeth McComas, age 78 of Harford County; Mary E. Dorsey of Baltimore who married Magruder Warfield in 1859; Mary E. Dorsey of Carroll County. This duplication of names demonstrates the difficulty of determining exactly which women are listed on a quilt.

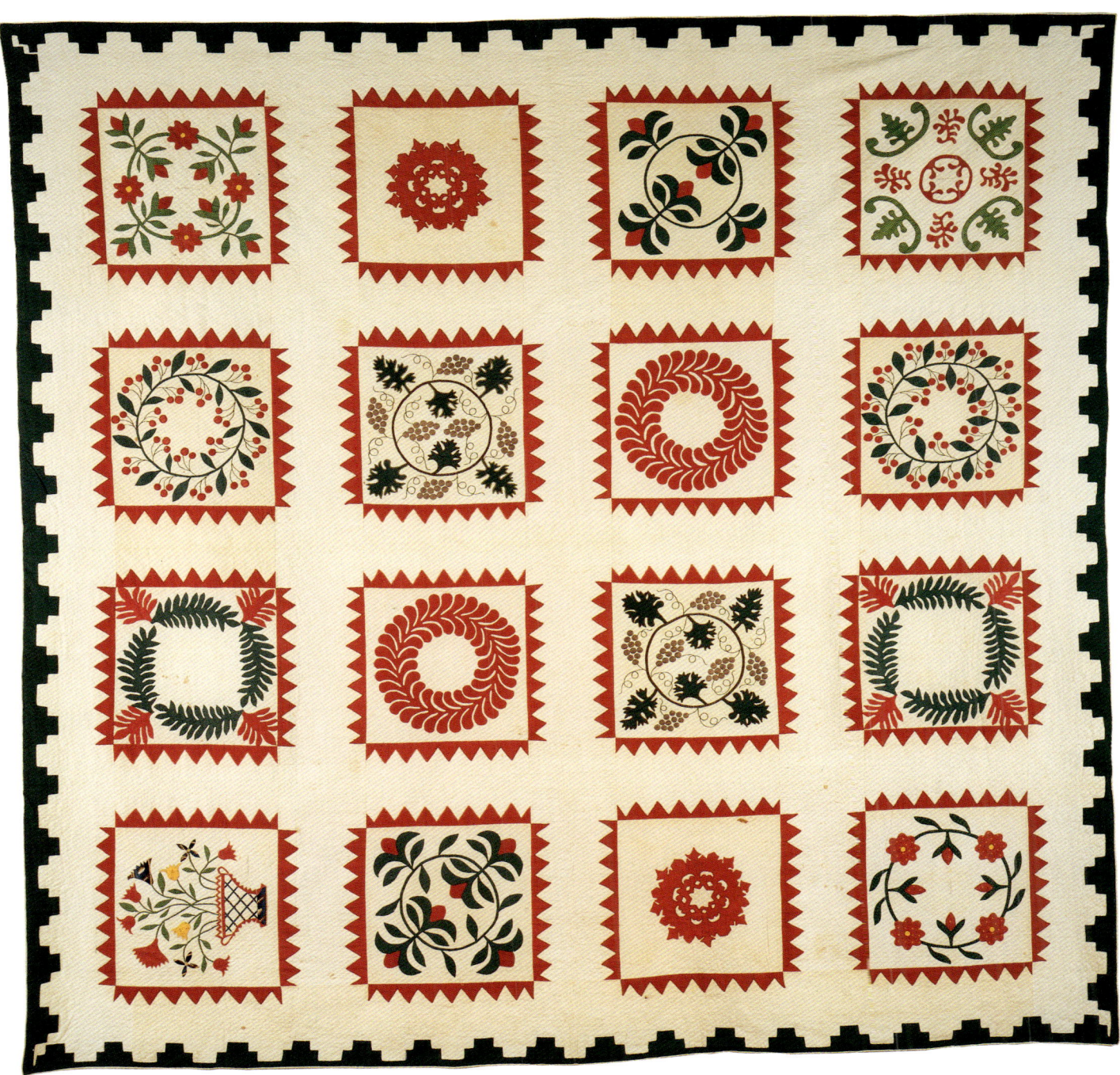

Catalogue 14
Baltimore Album Quilt
c. 1845-1850

Plain and printed cottons, white silk; cotton, silk, wool embroidery; inking; quilting 10 stitches to the inch.

Square size approximately 11 1/2 x 12 inches; quilt size approximately 98 1/4 x 106 1/4 inches.

Gift of Elizabeth Perry, 94.2

    This is a relatively early example of a quilt in the Designer II style, although the designs of a few of the simpler blocks may have been individually created by contributors to the quilt (see p. 23). Most of the squares and the border include such Designer II characteristics as heavily padded and embroidered single-piece roses, ruched flowers, wool-embroidered thorns and floral details, and a strong red-and-green color scheme. The red sawtooth sashing and inner border are partly pieced and partly appliquéd; the inner border is made of two similar but different pieces of Turkey-red cloth.

    This quilt abounds with interesting, albeit fragile, fabrics and unusual techniques. The elaboration of the border with many ruched flowers, intricately pleated fabric flowers, wool pom-pom flower centers, and other creative techniques is exceptional. The worn condition of the quilt permits us to determine that the maker stuffed the flowers as they were being appliquéd rather than through a slit in the back after the fabrics were stitched together. Among the many floral blocks are a temperance square and a spread-eagle square. One square has a central rectangle, which appears to have been sewn at a later date over a previous design. The rectangle originally had black embroidery, which has either disintegrated or been carefully picked out; the words *Holy Bible* may be discerned across the top of the rectangle. There is an inked inscription, *Sophia P. Cochran*, in square D6 and cross-stitched initials, *?EE*, in square B1.

Catalogue 15
Baltimore Album Quilt
c. 1848

Known to have belonged to a Mrs. Brown.

Plain and printed cottons, plain chintz, velvet; cotton, silk, wool embroidery; quilting 12 stitches to the inch.

Square size approximately 17 x 16 1/4 inches; quilt size approximately 111 1/2 x 108 1/2 inches.

Gift of Mrs. C. Creston Cathcart (great-granddaughter of Mrs. Brown), 70.19.1

    This quilt represents the style and needlework techniques of an anonymous designer, here referred to as Designer II, whose work appears frequently on Baltimore album quilts (see p. 23). Her work is characterized by a strongly red-and-green color scheme, three-dimensionality created by extra stuffing in some portions, or by flowers made of ruched tape, ribbon, or fabric, and by a reliance on wool and silk embroidery for highlights and details. Designer II did not employ the layered-appliqué technique for flowers; instead, most Designer II blossoms have a symmetrical "cookie-cutter" silhouette or the petals are defined by embroidery. The star block is probably a Mexican War period reference to the "Lone Star of Texas." Inscribed:
    B. F. Gress (square A1)
    L. D. Treadway (square D4).

Catalogue 16
Baltimore Album Quilt
c. 1849

Plain and printed cotton, velvet; silk and wool embroidery; inking; quilting 10 stitches to the inch.

Square size approximately 16 x 15 1/2 inches; quilt size approximately 101 x 96 3/4 inches.

The Designated Purchase Fund, 88.8

An especially bold and fine example of the Designer II style (see p. 23), this quilt features a memorial to Samuel Ringgold, a Maryland-born hero of the Mexican War. This square accurately reproduces the temporary monument, which was erected to the fallen cavalryman in the Merchants Exchange building in December 1848. The same monument appears on several other Baltimore album quilts but this is a particularly detailed and well-executed example. No printed depiction of the monument is known to survive; however, period newspapers printed excruciatingly detailed descriptions. The crossed keys emblem of trust in the topmost center square was used by both the Masons and Odd Fellows. This quilt, like Catalogue 15, has several squares that may have been cut from the same pattern but show evidence in the selection of thread and use of blind or a variety of decorative stitches of being sewn by different needlewomen. The only name on the quilt (square C2) is *Mrs. John Mann* who was born in 1790 and lived at 136 North Eutaw Street in Ward 12, Baltimore. Her husband was a farrier or blacksmith.

Catalogue 17
Baltimore Album Quilt
1845-1846

Chintz, plain and printed cottons, velvet, silk tape; silk and cotton embroidery and inking; quilting 7-10 stitches to the inch.

Square size approximately 16 1/2 x 16 1/2 inches; quilt size approximately 112 5/8 x 96 inches.

Gift of Mrs. George Davis Calvert, Jr. in memory of her mother Mrs. William Edmonds Gambrill, 73.103.1

    The names on this quilt include George M. Addison, born 1827, a lime dealer at 50 Conway Street and a member of the Methodist church; Susannah Harvey Addison, born 1803 and married 1821 to George C. Addison who was a shoe dealer; and Laura L. Dryden who lived at 332 1/2 Baltimore Street and who married merchant tailor James Salisbury in 1848. Another young woman whose name appears on the quilt is Mary M. Marshall who married James Price in 1853. E. C. McCauley is presumed to be Elizabeth Castel McCauley, the mother of Mary and Sarah McCauley who both worked on the quilt described as Catalogue 28 (see below). Several of the flower-vase squares appear to be the work of Designer II. The three-dimensional extension of the stuffed central cornucopia is extraordinary. The chintz border is a relatively early feature.

Catalogue 18
Baltimore Album Quilt
c. 1850

Made by Rachel Meyer (1818-1867)

Plain and printed cottons; silk and wool embroidery; quilting 16 stitches to the inch.

Center square size approximately 38 x 39 1/4 inches; small square size approximately 18 x 18 inches; quilt size approximately 99 x 101 inches.

Gift of Mrs. Alice F. Hecht, 70.56.1

    This intriguing quilt represents the style of a third major designer of Baltimore album quilts, here referred to as Designer III since her identity is unknown. The flowers on Designer III quilts are more stylized and exotic than those on other Baltimore album quilts; they often appear to have been derived from the fantasy flowers on chintzes and other oriental textiles. Designer III obviously delighted in animals of every sort. The two horsemen in the central square have sometimes been identified as George Washington and Andrew Jackson; however, they more likely represent Mexican War soldiers and may have been taken from illustrations in *Pictorial History of Mexico and the Mexican War* by John Frost, LL.D., published in Philadelphia in 1848. This book served as a model for other Designer III-style quilt squares (see Catalogue 19). The Christmas cactus square on the left is another Mexican reference, which appears on several Designer III quilts. This is one of the few Baltimore album quilts that has had extensive use; some of the fabrics were carefully replaced early in this century. Many Baltimore album quilts such as this one were enhanced with elaborate embroidery a generation or more before the crazy quilts of the 1890s featured such needlework.

Catalogue 19
Baltimore Album Quilt
c. 1850

Believed to have been made by Mrs. Josiah Goodman whose name is embroidered on the back along with the year 1850.

Plain and printed cottons, wool tweeds, velvet; wool and silk embroidery; quilting 15-16 stitches to the inch.

Square size approximately 16 x 16 1/2 inches; quilt size approximately 94 x 94 inches.

Gift of Mrs. Milford Nathan (granddaughter-in-law of Mrs. Goodman), 53.36.1

    The exotic nature of many of the appliquéd animals and the naturalistic appliquéd and embroidered insects scattered around the squares make this Designer III-style quilt amusing. The unusual color combinations and bold approach to the needlework may reflect influence from Mexican folk textiles. More obvious are the Mexican War references like the cavalryman discussed below. This quilt is greatly enriched by clever use of woolen fabrics and an abundance of embroidery stitches and types of thread. It is perhaps significant that Mr. Goodman was a clothier, and tweeds and woolens would have been part of his stock. Mrs. Goodman and her husband Josiah were both born in Germany; in Baltimore, they lived at 127 East Lombard Street. The Goodmans' daughter Emma was born in 1857 and Milford Nathan, husband of the donor, was her son.

    This quilt poses certain interesting identity problems. An extremely similar quilt was illustrated in an article by Julie Silber entitled "The Reiter Quilt: A Family Story in Cloth" in the first issue of *The Quilt Digest*, published in 1983. Family tradition ascribes that quilt, which had been cut into three pieces at some time, to a Jewish immigrant woman Liebe Gross Friedman and her daughter Katie Friedman Reiter working in McKeesport, Pennsylvania in the early 1890s. The author of the article admits that the lack of a quilting tradition in Slovakia where Mrs. Friedman was raised and where her daughter lived until the age of twelve, as well as the unusual style and symbolism of the quilt and its curious division into three parts pose attribution dilemmas.

    Both the Reiter quilt and the Goodman quilt have dashing horsemen appliqués cut from the same pattern which was undoubtedly adapted from the illustration of Captain Walker on page 213 of *A Pictorial History of Mexico and the Mexican War*, written by John Frost, LL.D. and published by Thomas, Cowperthwait & Co. in Philadelphia in 1848. Other similar quilts in the group also have designs that appear to have originated in this volume. During the past several years, at least six additional quilts related to both the Reiter quilt and the Maryland Historical Society's Goodman quilt have come to light. Other than the Reiter quilt, they all date to around 1848-1850 and have Maryland histories. We have continued to attribute the Goodman quilt to Maryland and to date it to circa 1850, the year embroidered on the back. Maryland Historical Society research has revealed that family histories for quilts often become confused or are missing the earliest parts of the stories; this may apply to the Reiter quilt. Additional information for related quilts may eventually illuminate the origins of this group of exceptional appliquéd quilts.

Catalogue 20
Baltimore Album Quilt
c. 1850

Plain and printed cottons; wool embroidery; quilting 12 stitches to the inch.

Square size approximately 16 x 16 inches; quilt size approximately 96 1/2 x 96 3/4 inches.

Gift of Mrs. Leslie Legum, 86.120

    This quilt was misdated for a number of years because of the brown print fabric from the 1930s, which was used to replace a deteriorated fabric in several squares. The central square reflects the influence of Mary Simon; the white-and-red rose wreath resembles Designer II's work; and a number of other squares are in Designer III's boldly embroidered style. The two different pineapples are creative variations on the same symbol of hospitality. The bird-nest-within-a-circle-of-birds is a charming design, which is known on just a few other Baltimore album quilts.

Catalogue 21
Baltimore Album Quilt
c. 1850

Plain and printed cottons; cotton, silk, wool embroidery; inking; quilting 9 stitches to the inch.

Square size approximately 16 1/4 x 16 1/4 inches; quilt size approximately 94 1/2 x 93 1/4 inches.

Gift of Mrs. Alexander Speer, 91.121

   This quilt includes a center square on which an unusual gathered technique was employed to create the roses. The basket of flowers within a floral wreath square is in the Mary Simon style, and there are several quite naturalistic floral bouquets along with very stylized ones. Like many Baltimore album quilts, this probably survived in unwashed condition until very recently when, regrettably, it was put through an automatic washing machine leading to great fabric destruction. It was rescued from a garbage can by the donor and has undergone expert conservation.

Catalogue 22
Baltimore Album Quilt Top
c. 1845

Plain and printed cottons; no quilting.

Center square size approximately 33 1/2 x 33 inches; small square size approximately 16 1/2 x 16 1/2 inches; quilt size approximately 98 1/2 x 100 1/2 inches.

Gift of Miss Irene Harmon, 30.1.1

The lack of quilting or sashing makes this quilt top look quite different, but it is organized like other early Baltimore album quilts with a central quadruple-sized square surrounded by symmetrically organized squares within border designs. The recurring leafy pinwheels give it a Pennsylvania German look to modern eyes. This quilt exemplifies the experimental phase, which merged the medallion style of quilt with the red-and-green block style to create the Baltimore album type. The feathery appliqué work is a high technical achievement. This quilt top seems to relate stylistically to a quilt, attributed to Mary Brown of Calvert County, Maryland, 1852, which sold at Christie, Manson & Woods International Inc., January 26, 1991 (New York, sale 7214, lot 196).

Many beautifully appliquéd Baltimore album quilt tops were left unfinished as testaments to the thousands of hours required for their completion or were finished into coverlets with a simple lining; today they are often called summer quilts or spreads.

Catalogue 23
Baltimore Album Quilt
1845-1848

Made for David Henry Crowl (1821-1906) by his mother Mary Celia Hiss Crowl (1789-1852), various female cousins, and four of his six sisters, Elizabeth (b. 1825), Martha (b. 1841), Susannah (d. 1847), Mary Celia (b. 1806).

Plain and printed cottons; wool embroidery and inking; quilting 8-10 stitches to the inch.

Square size approximately 16 3/8 x 16 1/2 inches; quilt size approximately 107 1/4 x 106 inches.

Gift of Philip W. Chase, Jr. (great-grandson of the recipient, D. H. Crowl), 93.1

    Family tradition calls this a freedom quilt, made for David Henry Crowl by his female relatives. There may be some historical confusion, however, since the tradition also relates that David and his father were in marine-related occupations, as symbolized by the beautiful central ship square, but the 1850 census lists both men as farmers in Baltimore County. Freedom quilts usually were presented when the recipient turned twenty-one and completed his apprenticeship; David was born in 1821 and married Caroline Greble in 1857. Perhaps the quilt was started to celebrate his twenty-first birthday but it is highly doubtful that some of the squares date before about 1848.

    Most of the squares are executed in the intricate and demanding "cut paper" technique. One of the most interesting squares is the log-cabin-and-cider-barrel motif from the 1840 Harrison-Tyler Presidential campaign (see p. 33). Two women, Sarah H. Childs and Joanna Richards, worked on both this quilt and the Batty quilt which was made in 1852 and is shown on page 120 of Dunton. According to Dunton, the Batty quilt was made for Isabelle Batty's marriage to Andrew Crow (incorrectly recorded for Crowl) who was David Henry Crowl's brother. The square on each quilt inscribed by Sarah H. Childs is a complex pictorial one with much inked detail. Sarah's name appears on the central ship square of this quilt and the hunting scene square on the Batty quilt; both are of the sort attributed to the designs of Mary Simon. The E. Hagerty whose name appears on square D1 of this quilt also inscribed square D4 of the Lipscomb quilt, which is number 11 (pages 92-93) in Katzenberg's catalogue. Inscribed names on this quilt include:

    Emeline C. Beam (square B5)

    Sarah H. Childs (square C3)

    Elizabeth J. Crowl (squares A1, A2), born 1824; lived at 58 York Avenue, Baltimore; married Thomas J. Taylor May 7, 1846, a butcher.

    Martha G. Crowl (squares A4, C1), born 1831.

    Susannah H. Crowl (squares A3, D3), born 1847.

    Emily Hagerty (square D1), married William Craig November 30, 1848, a tailor.

    Caroline K. Hiss (square C4), born 1829; lived at 43 Stiles Street, Baltimore; married Dennis C. Driscoll July 29, 1851, a variety storekeeper.

    Mary Celia Hiss (square B3), born 1829; lived at 43 Stiles Street; married Samuel Mulliken January 20, 1846, a dry goods dealer.

    Jemima Jessop (square C5), 1824-1858; member of a Methodist Church.

    Sarah Rebecca Jones (square E5), died 1863.

    Joanna Richards (squares B2, D5)

    Mary A. Scott (square B1), born 1818; lived at 157 Forest Street, Baltimore.

Catalogue 24
Baltimore Album Quilt
c. 1850

Made by Leonora Welch.

Plain and printed cottons; inking; quilting 9 stitches to the inch.

Square size approximately 16 x 16 1/2 inches; quilt size approximately 96 x 99 3/4 inches.

Gift of Mrs. J. Clinton Perrine (granddaughter of the maker's sister), 58.10.1

    Despite its frail condition, this quilt projects an appearance of ordered charm. Unfortunately, certain fabrics self-destruct over time because of chemicals in the dyes or mordants used in the dying and printing process. In addition to a number of individualistic squares, this quilt combines a fine central block in the style attributed to Mary Simon and squares designed or influenced by Designer II.

Catalogue 25
Maryland Album Quilt
c. 1846-1847

Presented to Methodist minister Thomas Harrison West Monroe by women from a variety of locations, primarily Hereford, Maryland; but also from as far away as Shippensburg, Pennsylvania; Harpers Ferry, Waterford, and Leesburg, Virginia; the District of Columbia; and Kaskaskia, Illinois. A number of the women from distant locations were related to those in the Hereford area and may have moved away after they had known Rev. Monroe in Maryland. Rev. Monroe served churches in a wide variety of locations between 1835 and 1860, and it also is possible that women in some of his early churches were asked to contribute to this quilt, which was probably put together following his service to the Columbia Street circuit in Baltimore during 1847.* It is not known for certain whether the name on a square indicates which woman actually made the square, or whether she had arranged or paid for it, or was being memorialized on it.

Chintz, plain and printed cottons; silk and cotton embroidery; inking; quilting 14 stitches to the inch.

Square size approximately 15 3/4 x 15 inches; quilt size approximately 105 x 105 inches.

Gift of Mr. and Mrs. Richard H. Green (descended from Rev. Monroe to Mr. Green through his stepmother), 94.9.1

This beautiful quilt strikingly illustrates the debt owed by Baltimore album quilts to the previous chintz appliquéd, or *broderie perse*, quilt style. Although often used to refer to any chintz-appliquéd American quilt, the English term *broderie perse* actually indicates a specific form of appliqué with additional embroidered enrichments. In addition to chintz-appliquéd squares, which were stuffed or embroidered, several squares on this quilt have calico appliquéd squares, which were enhanced with embroidery in the manner traditionally used with chintz.

The triangular red-and-blue design in the lower right square is the emblem of the Sons of Temperance, established in Maryland in 1844. The lengthy inscription within the wreath in the middle row is a quotation from the Biblical Book of Isaiah, LLI:7

How beautiful upon the mountains
are the feet of him that bringeth good
tidings that publisheth peace, that
bringeth good tidings of good, that publisheth
salvation
that sayeth unto Zion thy God reigneth.

Hereford lies directly between Baltimore and York, Pennsylvania; it is through this north-south route that the idea of elaborate, presentation album and friendship quilts probably moved from the Philadelphia area to Baltimore where it reached its zenith. The many names are executed in cross-stitch embroidery, exquisite free-hand inking, or with inked stamps of the sort more often found on Pennsylvania quilts than on Maryland examples. The inscribed names include:

Lenora Bosley (square B2)

Martha L. Bosley (square D1)

Mary Brown (square F2)

Susan Cahoon (square E3)

Margaret Cridler (square E4)

Ann Rebecca Donavin (square F6)

Continued on page 98

Ann Gailey (square E6), born 1813, a milliner of Baltimore County, Maryland

Jemima Howard (square C1), 1822-1898, who married Archibald Lamar

Harriet Hughes (square C6), of Harpers Ferry, Virginia

Jane Kelly (square A4)

Ann M. King (square E2), of Harpers Ferry, Virginia

Jane A. Lewis (square F1)

Mary B. Matthews (square D5), born 1807, married to Benjamin Matthews, a farmer in Baltimore County, Maryland

Tabitha W. Matthews (square C2), of Hereford, Maryland

Martha A. McCoy (square B1), of Harpers Ferry, Virginia

Mrs. Ann Merryman (square B3), born 1786, widow of Nicholas Merryman, Jr., a farmer at "Bacon Hall," Baltimore County, Maryland

Margaret S. Miller (square E1), of Washington City (D.C.)

Catherine Monroe (square E5), of Hereford, Maryland

Sarah A. Moor(e) (square B4), of Harpers Ferry, Virginia

Charlotte Jane Morton (square A2), who married Joshua A. Tipton in 1849, of Hereford, Maryland

Martha Eliza Morton (square A5), born 1804, maiden name Merryman, married to Dixon Morton in 1826, a merchant of Hereford, Maryland

Elizabeth Noris (square F3)

Mary E. Norwood (square A6), of Leesburg, Virginia

Lydia Wells Orrick (square D4), maiden name Kirk, married in 1832 to Dr. John C. Orrick of Hereford, Maryland

Mary C. Perry (square B5), of Kaskaskia, Illinois

Catherine B. Price (square D2), born 1792, married to Samuel D. Price, a merchant of Hereford, Maryland

Mary Price (square B6)

Susan R. Price (square D6), born 1828, daughter of Catherine B. Price (see above), of Hereford, Maryland

Edith M. Rabe (square A3), of Hereford, Maryland

Agnes Rankin (square C5), of Baltimore, Maryland

Mary Tinley (square A1)

Esther Tipton (square C3), of Hereford, Maryland

Jane Tipton (square D3), of Hereford, Maryland

Margaret Towner (square F4), of Waterford, Virginia

Mary C. Warfield (square F5), probably niece of Sarah Warfield, wife of Rev. T. H. W. Monroe for whom quilt was made; married a Slingluff in 1851, of Sams Creek, Carroll County, Maryland

S. Worthington (square C4)

* According to Rev. Edwin Schell, Executive Secretary, Methodist Historical Society, Rev. Monroe's appointments were:

    Harpers Ferry (now West Virginia), 1835-1836

    Winchester, Virginia, 1837-1838

    Liberty (Frederick County), Maryland, 1839-1840

    Patapsco (Ellicott City), Maryland, 1841-1842

    Berkeley (now West Virginia), 1843

    Chambersburg, Pennsylvania, 1846

    Baltimore City, Columbia Street Station, 1847

    Harpers Ferry (now West Virginia), 1848-1849

    Huntington, Pennsylvania, 1850-1853

    Frederick, Maryland, 1854-1857

    Baltimore Circuit, Maryland, 1858

    Baltimore City, Franklin Street Station, 1859-1860

Catalogue 26
Baltimore Album Quilt
1850

Made by Mrs. Stephen MacDonald (née Sarah Jane Trigg) of Ellicott City and, after 1868, of Baltimore.

Plain and printed cottons, velvet; silk and wool embroidery; quilting 12 stitches to the inch.

Square size approximately 17 3/4 x 17 3/4 inches; quilt size approximately 102 3/8 x 103 5/8 inches.

Gift of Mrs. Martha King (daughter of Sarah Trigg MacDonald), 48.68.1

The squares and vine border of this quilt were well executed and their designs were heavily influenced by the finest Baltimore album quilts. However, none of the designs for this quilt are as sophisticated as the squares attributed directly to Mary Simon, Designer II, or Designer III. Several squares and the border resemble Designer II's work and the awkwardly drawn spread-eagle also appears on other Baltimore album quilts. The similarity between some of the designs on this quilt and some on Catalogue 27 may indicate that there were simple patterns that circulated among Baltimore women or that there were quilt designers or kit makers who worked in a less fully-developed manner than the readily identified style attributed to Mary Simon, Designer II, or Designer III. The narrow sashing crowds the squares, which have been thoughtfully organized with the most complex designs at the top of the quilt.

Catalogue 27
Baltimore Album Quilt
c. 1840s

Made by Mrs. George Vineyard (née Margaret Meyer).

Chintz, plain and printed cottons; cotton embroidery; quilting 7-9 stitches to the inch.

Square size approximately 16 1/2 x 16 1/2 inches; quilt size approximately 94 3/4 x 94 3/4 inches.

Gift of Mrs. Maurice D. Laupeimer (great-granddaughter of Margaret Meyer Vineyard), 69.18.1

Several of the squares of this pleasing Baltimore album quilt depict the same imagery as squares on the quilt made by Mrs. MacDonald (see Catalogue 26). Although far simpler than many prized Baltimore album quilts, this quilt is carefully balanced and preserves a sense of graphic vitality appropriate to its two-dimensional fabric medium. The hearts-and-hand square may symbolize Odd Fellows membership or affiliation with some other benevolent society.

Catalogue 28
Baltimore Album Quilt Top
c. 1848

Plain and printed cotton; inking; no quilting.

Square size approximately 17 1/4 x 17 1/4 inches; quilt size approximately 79 3/4 x 80 1/2 inches.

Gift of Mrs. Clara H. Bishop, 88.101

    Most of the squares of this quilt top have designs, which completely fill the space. The complex basket of fruit surrounded by flowers in the bottom row presents yet another way to layer fabric scraps to resemble the multiple petals of a rose blossom. The red-and-green crossed branches in each corner tie this quilt to the earlier red-and-green style of appliquéd quilts in which the same pattern appears in all the squares. The tan fabric in the lower flower basket placed diagonally was probably originally green with a fugitive blue dye, which has vanished.

    The machine stitching connecting the squares indicates that they were assembled some years after the appliqué work was done. Names on this quilt include:

    Almi? B?? (square B1)

    Mrs. Manifold (square A3)

    Jane A. Hipsley (square B4), born in 1838, of the second district, Baltimore County

    Malvina Hipsley (square D4), born in 1833, of the second district, Baltimore County, who married John G. Holland in 1859

    Kate L. Holland (square A2)

    Mary E. Harrison (square C4)

    Mary (square C3), born 1834, *Ruth A.*, (square B3), and *Sarah A.* (square D2), born 1836 *McCauley*. Mary and Sarah are presumed to be the daughters of Elizabeth Castel McCauley who is believed to have worked on the quilt discussed as Catalogue 17 (see above)

Catalogue 29
Baltimore Album Quilt
c. 1845-1846

Made for Benjamin Almony (b. 1825) at the time of his twenty-first birthday.

Plain and printed cottons; quilting 12 stitches to the inch.

Square size approximately 15 1/2 x 15 1/4 inches; quilt size approximately 78 x 77 inches.

Gift of Mrs. Mabel Kelbaugh (granddaughter of Benjamin Almony), 68.109.1

The typical, Baltimore album quilt squares of this quilt are somewhat overpowered by the red and yellow printed calico borders, which were added in the twentieth century. This quilt was made as a freedom quilt when the recipient reached his legal majority and became "free" of his apprenticeship. As with the quilt made for David Crowl (Catalogue 23), the imagery on the quilt implies an involvement of the recipient in the maritime trade, but the 1850 census lists both Benjamin and his father as farmers. The naive sailing ship square is particularly charming. Benjamin was from Harford County, and this quilt exemplifies the simplification that prevailed outside the immediate urban setting.

Catalogue 30
Baltimore Album Quilt
c. 1850; c. 1880; 1918

Most of the squares of this quilt were made around 1850; a generation later, a border strip was made but not completed; the quilt was assembled in 1918 by friends of Mrs. John Worley at the time of her marriage. The border was used as vertical sashing and cut to form the two upper corner squares.

Plain and printed cottons, plain chintz, silk, wool; silk and wool embroidery; quilting 7-8 stitches to the inch.

Square size approximately 17 x 17 inches; quilt size approximately 93 7/8 x 79 1/8 inches.

Gift of Philip A. Beatty, 48.76.2

This vibrant quilt shows evidence of work by three different generations of needlewomen, yet it remains unfinished. The early squares are in the manner of Designer II with exceptionally rich embroidery. The later vine border strips, used as sashing and corner squares, employ embroidery to represent the stems and vines, which would have been appliquéd on mid-century examples. Although the fabrics and patterns for the flowers have been carefully matched to the older squares, they are not the same. The 1918 assembly was accomplished with a strong sense of design and great respect for the squares, which by then were about seventy years old.

Almost hidden among the red and white roses in the middle right square are the three-link chain and crossed keys of Odd Fellows membership. The six-pointed yellow star surrounded by arrows, flags, and an eagle and shield may be a Mexican War reference; six-pointed stars are easier to draw and cut than five-pointed ones. The number of stars on Baltimore album quilt flags seem to have depended on the skill of the needlewoman rather than the number of states in the Union.

Catalogue 31
Maryland Album Quilt
1862

Made by a number of women in Harford County, Maryland, for Joseph Levin Mills (1840-1924).

Plain and printed cottons; inking; quilting 5-6 stitches to the inch.

Square size approximately 16 1/2 x 16 3/4 inches; quilt size approximately 81 3/4 x 80 3/4 inches.

Gift of Katherine Elizabeth (Steele) Koch (great-granddaughter of Joseph Mills), 93.17.1

    The year 1862 was particularly noteworthy for young Joseph Mills. His tiny pocket diary records, with meticulous handwriting, the presentation of this quilt to him on March 3 with a speech by Mrs. Michael representing the numerous ladies who had worked on it. Mills was ordained to the Methodist ministry on March 16 and married November 25, 1862. Joseph's first church assignment as minister was in Newton, Worcester County.
    A nice sense of balance has been maintained in the arrangement of similar but not identical squares. This is one of the latest true Baltimore album quilts; only one square breaks the entirely red-and-green color scheme by including blue and yellow. By 1862, the custom of presenting an album quilt to a minister was at least two decades old, and the great fad for the finest Baltimore album quilts had waned almost ten years earlier. The time, money, and fabric restrictions occasioned by the Civil War put an end to numerous women indulging in this sort of quilting until it was revived in the 1980s. Inscribed names, all thought to be from Harford County, include:
    Lucritia C. Barren (square B5), 1818-1887, member of an Episcopal Church.
    Lizzie Cronin (square E3), 1830-1899, married Benjaman F. Cronin, a farmer; member of a Presbyterian Church.
    Mollie L. Gallup (probably Mary Louise Gallup) (square E1); member of an Episcopal Church.
    Kate Holloway (square A5)
    Rachel E. Hoopman (squares A3, B3), 1824-1918, married Amos Osborn; member of a Presbyterian Church.
    Matise M. Martin (square E2)
    Maria G. McClure (square A2), born 1840.
    Ella Michael (square C2)
    Mary E. Mitchell (square C4), born 1838, daughter of a farmer.
    Louise Murphy (square D5)
    Sallie J. Numbers (square E4), born 1831, daughter of a shoemaker.
    Sallie E. Osborne (squares C5, D3)
    Kate Ramtican (square C1)
    Kp? Razort? (square B4)
    Mrs. Taylor (square B2)
    Maggie Taylor (square B4)
    Mollie Taylor (squares A1, D4)
    R. Elliner Taylor (square D1)
    George T.(or Y) Walker (square D2), born 1773, census lists as deaf.
    A. Yain? (square E5)

Catalogue 32
Seven Unfinished Quilt Squares
c. 1850

Found in a trunk, which had belonged to Mary Evans of Baltimore (c. 1833-1916; later Mrs. John Ford of New York state)

Plain and printed cottons; cotton and wool embroidery; inking; no quilting.

Quadruple-sized center square size approximately 38 1/8 x 38 inches; average small square size 17 x 17 inches.

The Emilie McKim Reed Memorial Purchase Fund, 90.11.1-7

Individual quilt squares in the Baltimore album quilt style turn up with some regularity in old trunks and chests. It is often hard to determine whether these squares were made by the person who once owned them or whether they were gifts to that person. It was this group of squares, examined and photographed by Dr. William R. Dunton, Jr., early in this century, which prompted the theory that Mary Evans may have been responsible for creating many of the finest Baltimore album quilts. Although the squares remained in the family until 1990, they were unseen by scholars for about six decades. Dr. Dunton's photograph of the large, basted City Spring square was illustrated in his 1946 *Old Quilts* and in Dena Katzenberg's 1981 *Baltimore Album Quilts*, leading to great speculation about Miss Evans.

The census records for 1850 indicate that Mary was seventeen at that time and that she lived in a household headed by her widowed mother and including at least two older brothers with their young wives and children. Mary herself did not wed until rather late in life, and there is no other evidence of her involvement with fancy needlework. There are far too many quilt squares in the style of the City Spring and Rev. John Hall blocks for such a young girl to have been responsible for making them all within a brief six-to-eight year period starting when she would have been only fourteen or fifteen years old. In addition, close examination of such squares indicates that, although they contain the same or similar fabrics, they often reveal very different needlework.

When this group of squares was acquired by the Maryland Historical Society, it was realized that they represent both the design aesthetics and needle skills of at least three or four different women. Since the largest square is not appliquéd and the others differ so greatly, we have no way of determining if Mary Evans worked on any of these pieces. We now attribute the Rev. John Hall square and the City Spring square to the design work of Mary Simon; the City Spring square may provide evidence of the cut and basted state in which Mrs. Simon's squares were distributed (see p. 17). Several of the squares have inked inscriptions: *Margarett A. Stansbury* on the four-part square with buds design; *Mrs. Catharine A. Boyd* on the cornucopia square; *Mrs. Ann M. Bruscup* on the berry-and-leaf-heart square; *John Hall* on the figural square; and *Nathaniel Lee* on the Odd Fellow square. The inked handwriting differs from square to square but much of it is especially fine.

115

Catalogue 33
Two Individual Baltimore Album Quilt Squares
c. 1849

Ringgold square inscribed by Cynthia Duvall of New Market, Maryland; possibly made from a Baltimore "kit."

Square size approximately 16 3/4 x 16 1/2 inches.

The Mrs. F. J. Klein Purchase Fund, 90.49.1-.2

These two squares are from a group of three found in New Market, Maryland; however, both show evidence of originating in Baltimore. The third square, which was not acquired by the Maryland Historical Society, is a rather simple, chintz flower sprig appliqué.

The flag square employs the blue rainbow fabric so prevalent in Baltimore album quilts, and parts of the square are executed in the reverse appliqué technique considered to be one of the "hallmarks" of Baltimore's mid-nineteenth-century quilts. The inscription comes from the fourth verse of the "Star-Spangled Banner," which must have been little-known outside Baltimore, where it was written in 1814. The song was not adopted as the national anthem until 1931. This square may be merely patriotic or may have deeper political significance. The influx of German and Irish immigrants after 1844 resulted in the emergence of what was variously called the "Native American" or "Know Nothing" political party, which was largely aligned with the Democrats. What started as underground opposition to new immigration was fostered by several secret fraternal societies. This organization was particularly strong in Maryland and fueled the many Baltimore riots and mob scenes of the 1850s. In 1853, the "Know Nothings" formally designated themselves the "Order of the Star-Spangled Banner," and by 1856 this party had elected a Maryland governor and gained control of the Baltimore City Council.*

The monument square is in honor of Major Samuel Ringgold, a Maryland hero of the Mexican War. This square, depicting a temporary monument erected in the Merchants Exchange building, appears on at least eight surviving Baltimore album quilts (see Catalogue 16). The position of the eagle on this square helps substantiate the basted "kit" theory about the origin of some Baltimore album quilt squares. On the other known Ringgold monument squares, the eagle is perched on top of the monument; here, it is easy to conjecture that if this square left Baltimore for New Market as a basted kit, only one or two stitches needed to have come loose for the eagle to have fallen off. Perhaps the recipient, not knowing its proper position, simply placed it in an empty space. The square is inscribed:

Sacred to/the memory of Major Ringgold/When
the gallant Ringgold received the wound/at
the battle of Palo Alto, which deprived the army/
of one of its brightest ornaments, some of his/
comrades gathered around him, when he/intoned
"Leave me to my fate there is/much for every man to do"
Cynthia Duvall/New Market/Frederick County/Maryland

* see Kahn, Philip, Jr. *A Stitch in Time: The Four Seasons of Baltimore's Needle Trades*, 21.

Catalogue 34
Maryland Album-Type Crib Quilt
c. 1843

Made by Margaret Boyce Elliott.

Plain and printed cotton; embroidery; quilting 9 stitches to the inch.

Square size approximately 15 x 15 inches; quilt size approximately 42 3/4 x 43 1/2 inches.

Gift of J. Carroll Stow and Mrs. Helen Stow Duker (great-grandchildren of the maker), 44.88.1

    This charming, red-and-green crib quilt is an album by virtue of the fact that the designs of the squares differ. Careful genealogical research leads to the conclusion that the quilt probably was originally made for Margaret Elliott's granddaughter Margaret Jane Collins who was born in 1843. It was later inscribed with the initials and birth date of Margaret Jane's son Charles Mortimer Stow who was born in 1865. One square is embroidered Margaret Elliott for the maker; one is embroidered in a different hand MAC for Mrs. Elliott's daughter Mary Ann (Elliott) Collins, mother of the recipient Margaret Jane Collins; one square is embroidered *CMS/1865* for Margaret Jane's son Charles Mortimer Stow; the fourth square is embroidered 1865. The family heirloom traditions of quilts often lead to confusion as to maker and date when a cherished quilt passes through several generations of use.

Selected Bibliography

Allen, Gloria Seaman. *Old Line Traditions: Maryland Women and Their Quilts.* Washington, D. C.: DAR Museum, 1985.

—. *First Flowerings: Early Virginia Quilts.* Washington, D. C.: DAR Museum, 1987.

America's Quilts Created by the Country's Best Quilters. Lincolnwood, IL: Publications International, Ltd., 1990.

An Account of the Grand Celebration of the Independent Order of Odd-Fellows. Baltimore, MD: Sands and Neilson, 1831.

Arkansas Quilter's Guild, Inc. *Arkansas Quilts, Arkansas Warmth.* Paducah, KY: American Quilter's Society, 1987.

Arthur, T. S., ed. *The Crystal Fount for All Seasons.* New York: Cornish, Lambert & Co., 1850.

—. *The Temperance Gift.* New York: Leavitt & Allen, 1834.

Atkins, Jacqueline M., and Phyllis A. Tepper. *New York Beauties: Quilts from the Empire State.* New York: Dutton Studio Books, 1992.

Bank, Mirra. *Anonymous Was A Woman.* New York: St. Martin's Press, 1979.

Barber, Rita Barrow. *Somewhere in Between: Quilts and Quilters of Illinois.* Paducah, KY: American Quilter's Society, 1986.

Benberry, Cuesta Ray, and Carol Pinney Crabb. *A Patchwork of Pieces: An Anthology of Early Quilt Stories, 1845-1940.* Paducah, KY: American Quilter's Society, 1993.

Bennett, Ellie, Frances Bittle, Doris Leas, et al. *The Hands That Made Them: Quilts of Adams County, Pennsylvania.* Camp Hill, PA: Adams County Quilt Documentation Committee, 1993.

Bespangled, Painted and Embroidered: Decorated Masonic Aprons in America, 1790-1850. Lexington, Massachusetts: Museum of Our National Heritage, 1980.

Beyer, Jinny. *The Art and Technique of Creating Medallion Quilts Including a Rich Collection of Historic and Contemporary Examples.* McLean, VA: EPM Publications, Inc., 1982.

Bishop, Robert. *New Discoveries in American Quilts.* New York: E. P. Dutton and Co., Inc., 1975.

Bishop, Robert, and Carter Houck. *All Flags Flying: American Patriotic Quilts as Expressions of Liberty.* New York: E. P. Dutton, 1986.

Blum, Dilys, and Jack L. Lindsey. *Nineteenth-Century Appliqué Quilts.* Bulletin, Vol. 85, no. 362-364. Philadelphia, PA: Philadelphia Museum of Art, 1989.

Bowman, Doris M. *The Smithsonian Treasury of American Quilts.* Washington, D. C.: Smithsonian Institution Press, 1991.

Boylan, Anne M. *Sunday School, The Formation of an American Institution, 1790-1880.* New Haven: Yale University Press, 1988.

Brackman, Barbara. *Clues in the Calico: A Guide to Identifying and Dating Antique Quilts.* San Francisco, CA: EPM Publications, Inc., 1989.

—. *Encyclopedia of Appliqué.* McLean, VA: EPM Publications, Inc., 1993.

—. "Turkey Red: the Quilter's Favorite Fabric." Lecture at the Maryland Historical Society, Baltimore, MD, November 12, 1993.

Brackman, Barbara, Jennie A. Chinn, Gayle R. Davis, et al. *Kansas Quilts and Quilters.* Lawrence, Kansas: University Press of Kansas, 1993.

Bridif, Josette. *Printed French Fabrics: Toiles de Jouy.* New York: Rizzoli, 1989.

Bresenhan, Karoline Patterson, and Nancy O'Bryant Puentes. *Lone Stars: A Legacy of Texas Quilts, 1836-1936.* Vol. 1. Austin, TX: University of Texas Press, 1986.

Brugger, Robert J. *Maryland: A Middle Temperament, 1634-1980.* Baltimore, MD: The Johns Hopkins University Press, 1988.

Bullard, Lacy Folmar. *Quilts, From Colonial to Contemporary.* Lincolnwood, IL: Publications International, Ltd., 1992.

Bullard, Lacy Folmar, and Betty Jo Shiell. *Chintz Quilts: Unfading Glory.* Tallahassee, Florida: Serendipity Publishers, 1983.

Bunker, Gary L. "Ante-bellum Caricature and Women's Sphere." *Journal of Women's History* 3, no. 3 (Winter, 1992).

Callcott, George H. *Mary and Political Behavior: Four Centuries of*

Political Culture. Baltimore, MD: Maryland Historical Society, 1986.

Chambers-Shiller, Lee Virginia. *Liberty a Better Husband: Single Women in America: the Generations of 1780-1840*. New Haven: Yale University Press, 1984.

Clark, Ricky, George W. Knepper, and Ellice Ronsheim. *Quilts in Community: Ohio's Traditions*. Nashville, TN: Rutledge Hill Press, 1991.

Clarke, S. R. "Report of the Board of Health." Baltimore: Health Office, 1851.

Clement, J., ed. *Eight Thousand Noble Deeds of American Women*. Buffalo, N. Y.: George H. Derby and Co., 1852.

Cleveland, Richard L., and Donna Bister. *Plain and Fancy: Vermont's People and Their Quilts as a Reflection of America*. Gualala, CA: The Quilt Digest Press, 1991.

Coale Collection, MS. 248. Manuscripts Division, Maryland Historical Society Library.

Cochran, Rachel, Rita Erickson, Natalie Hart, and Barbara Schaffer. *New Jersey Quilts, 1777-1950: Contributions to an American Tradition*. Paducah, KY: American Quilter's Society, 1992.

Crews, Patricia Cox, and Ronald C. Naugle. *Nebraska Quilts and Quiltmakers*. Lincoln, Nebraska: University of Nebraska Press, 1991.

Croce, Ann Jerome. "A Woman Outside Her Time: Elizabeth Barstow Stoddard (1823-1910) and 19th Century American Popular Fiction." *Women's Studies* 19 (1991).

Cross, Mary Bywater. *Treasures in the Trunk: Quilts of the Oregon Trail*. Nashville, TN: Turledge Hill Press, Inc., 1993.

de Dillmont, Therese. *Encyclopedia of Needlework*. rev. ed. New York: Crown Publishers, Inc., 1987.

Dobbin Family Papers, MS. 2385. Manuscripts Division, Maryland Historical Society Library.

Done Notebooks, MS. 306. Manuscripts Division, Maryland Historical Society Library.

Duke, Dennis, and Deborah Harding, eds. *America's Glorious Quilts*. New York: Hugh Lauter Levin Associates, Inc. 1987.

Dunton, William Rush, Jr., M. D. *Old Quilts*. Catonsville, MD: William R. Dunton, Jr., M. D., 1946.

Duryea, Joseph T., D. D., ed. *The Presbyterian Hymnal*. Philadelphia, PA: Presbyterian Board of Publication, 1874.

Elbert, E. Duane, and Rachel Kamm. *History From the Heart: Quilt Paths Across Illinois*. Nashville, TN: Rutledge Hill Press, 1993.

Ferrero, Pat, Elaine Hedges, and Julie Silber. *Hearts and Hands: the Influence of Women and Quilts on American Society*. San Francisco, CA: The Quilt Digest Press, 1987.

Finley, Ruth E. *Old Patchwork Quilts and the Women Who Made Them*. rev. ed. McLean, VA: EPM Publications, Inc., 1992.

Fox, Sandi. *Small Endearments: Nineteenth-Century Quilts for Children*. New York: Charles Scribner's Sons, 1985.

—. *Wrapped in Glory: Figurative Quilts and Bedcovers, 1700-1900*. New York: Thames and Hudson, Inc., 1991.

Franco, Barbara. *Fraternally Yours: A Decade of Collecting*. Lexington, Massachusetts: Museum of Our National Heritage, 1986.

Frost, Helen Young, and Pam Knight Stevenson. *Grand Endeavors: Vintage Arizona Quilts and Their Makers*. Flagstaff, AZ: Northland Publishing Co., 1992.

Frost, John, LL.D. *A Pictorial History of Mexico and the Mexican War*. Philadelphia, PA: Thomas Cowperthwait and Co., 1848.

Fry, Gladys-Marie. *Stitched From the Soul: Slave Quilts from the Ante-Bellum South*. New York: Dutton Studio Books, 1990.

Gamse, Erin E. "The Influence of Fraternal Organizations on Baltimore Album Quilt Designs." Master's thesis, Cooperstown Graduate Program, State University of New York, College at Oneonta, 1994.

Glickman, Gena Debra. "A Study of the Role of Women in the Transformation of the Curriculum at the Maryland Institute of Mechanic Arts from 1825-1875." Dissertation submitted to the University of Maryland, 1992.

Godey, Louis A., and Mrs. Sarah J. Hale, eds. "The Sphere of Woman. Translated from the German of Goethe." *Godey's Magazine and Lady's Book* (1850): 209.

Godey, Louis A., and Mrs. Sarah J. Hale, eds. *Godey's Lady's Book and Ladies' American Magazine*. (Philadelphia, PA: 1839-1855).

Goldman, Marilyn, Marguerite Wiebusch, et al. *Quilts of Indiana: Crossroads of Memories*. Indianapolis, IN: Indiana University Press, 1991.

Graves Papers, MS. 407. Manuscripts Division, Maryland Historical Society Library.

Graves, Mrs. A. J. *Woman in America, Being an Examination into the Moral and Intellectual Condition of American Female Society*. New York: Harper and Brothers, 1842.

Green, Harvey. *The Light of the Home: An Intimate View of the Lives of Women in Victorian America*. New York: Pantheon Books, 1983.

Handler, Mimi. "Masonic Symbols: Decorating Our History" *Early American Life* 24, no. 4 (August 1993).

Hannah Mary Trimble Papers. MS. 2517. Manuscripts Division, Maryland Historical Society Library.

Harnden, Jane Amstutz, and Pamela Frazee Woolbright. *Oklahoma Heritage Quilts*. Paducah, KY: American Quilter's Society, 1990.

Harris, Jennifer, ed. *Textiles, 5,000 Years: An International History and Illustrated Survey*. New York: Harry N. Abrams, Inc., 1993.

Havig, Bettina. *Missouri Heritage Quilts*. Paducah, KY: American Quilter's Society, 1986.

Hefford, Wendy. *The Victoria and Albert Museum's Textile Collection: Design for Printed Textiles in England from 1750 to 1850*. New York: Canopy Books, 1992.

Helms, Winfred G., ed. *Notable Maryland Women*. 1977.

Henson, George W., D. D., ed. *Gospel Songs and Hymns We Love*. Philadelphia, PA: Theodore Presser Co., 1944.

Herbert, J. C. "An Address Delivered at the First Anniversary Meeting of the Maryland State Temperance Society." Annapolis, MD: Printed by J. Green (January 5, 1832).

Higgins, Edwin. *A Compilation of Maryland Laws of Interest to Women*. Baltimore: Press of Baltimore Methodist, 1897.

Hinson, Dolores A. *American Graphic Quilt Designs*. New York: Arco Publishing, Inc., 1983.

Hoffman, Lynn T. *Patterns in Time: Quilts of Western New York*. Buffalo, N. Y.: Buffalo and Erie County Historical Society, 1990.

Hoffman, Victoria. *Quilts: A Window to the Past*. North Andover, Massachusetts: Museum of American Textile History, 1991.

Hoke, Donald. *Dressing the Bed: Quilts and Coverlets from the Collections of the Milwaukee Public Museum*. Milwaukee, WI: Milwaukee Public Museum, 1985.

Holstein, Jonathan. *The Pieced Quilt, An American Design Tradition*. New York: Galahad Books, 1973.

Holstein, Jonathan, and John Finley. *Kentucky Quilts, 1800-1900: The Kentucky Quilt Project*. New York: Pantheon Press, 1982.

Homage to Amanda: Two Hundred Years of American Quilts from the Collection of Edwin Binney, 3rd and Gail Binney-Winslow. San Francisco, CA: R K Press, 1984.

Hornback, Nancy. *Quilts in Red and Green: The Flowering of Folk Design in Nineteenth Century America*. Wichita, KS: The Wichita/Sedgwick County Historical Museum, 1992.

Horton, Laurel, and Lynn Robertson Myers. *Social Fabric: South Carolina's Traditional Quilts*. Columbia, S. C.: McKissick Museum, n. p.

Houck, Carter. *The Quilt Encyclopedia Illustrated*. New York: Harry N. Abrams, Inc., 1991.

Howard, William Travis, Jr., M. D. *Public Health Administration and the Natural History of Disease in Baltimore, Maryland, 1797-1920*.

Ingleside Seminary: A Home School for Young Ladies. Baltimore: Henry E. Huber, 1859

James, Ardis, and Penny McMorris. *Quilts: The James Collection*, n. p.

Jane Townsend Quigg Letters, MS. 1926. Manuscripts Division, Maryland Historical Society Library.

Jane Townsend Quigg Papers, MS. 1926. Manuscripts Division, Maryland Historical Society.

Jerde, Judith. *Encyclopedia of Textiles*. New York: Facts on File, Inc., 1992.

Jessop Family Papers, MS. 2345. Manuscripts Division, Maryland Historical Society Library.

Kahn, Philip, Jr. *A Stitch in Time: The Four Seasons of Baltimore's Needle Trades*. Baltimore, MD: Maryland Historical Society, 1989.

Katzenberg, Dena S. *The Great American Cover-Up: Counterpanes of the Eighteenth and Nineteenth Centuries*. Baltimore, MD: The Baltimore Museum of Art, 1971.

—. *Baltimore Album Quilts*. Baltimore, MD: The Baltimore Museum of Art, 1982.

Kimball, Jeana. *Reflections of Baltimore*. Bothell, WA: That Patchwork Place, 1989.

—. *Red and Green: An Appliqué Tradition*. Bothell, WA: That Patchwork Place, 1990.

Kiracofe, Roderick. *The American Quilt: A History of Cloth and Comfort 1750-1950*. New York Clarkson Potter, Publishers, 1993.

Kleeblatt, Norman L., and Gerard C. Wertkin. *The Jewish Heritage in American Folk Art*. New York: Universe Books, 1984.

Klimaszewski, Cathy Rosa. *Made to Remember: American Commemorative Quilts*. Ithaca, N. Y.: Herbert F. Johnson Museum of Art, 1991.

Kolter, Jane Bently. *Forget Me Not: A Gallery of Friendship and Album Quilts*. Pittstown, N. J.: The Main Street Press, Inc., 1985.

Lasansky, Jeannette. *In the Heart of Pennsylvania*. Lewisburg, PA: Oral Traditions Project of the Union County Historical Society, 1985.

—. ed. *In the Heart of Pennsylvania: Symposium Papers*. Lewisburg, PA: Oral Traditions Project of the Union County Historical Society, 1986.

—. *Pieced by Mother: Over 100 Years of Quiltmaking Traditions*. Lewisburg, PA: Oral Traditions Project of the Union County Historical Society, 1987.

—. ed. *Pieced by Mother: Symposium Papers*. Lewisburg, PA: Oral Traditions Project of the Union County Historical Society, 1988.

—. *Bits and Pieces, Textile Traditions*. Lewisburg, PA: Oral Traditions Project of the Union County Historical Society, 1991.

—. ed. *On the Cutting Edge: Textile Collectors, Collections, and Traditions*. Lewisburg, PA: Oral Traditions Project of the Union County Historical Society, 1994.

Laury, Jean Ray. *Ho For California! Pioneer Women and Their Quilts*. New York: E. P. Dutton, 1990.

Lea, Elizabeth E. *Domestic Cookery: Useful Receipts and Hints to Young Housekeepers*. Baltimore: Cushing & Brothers, 1846.

Lipsett, Linda Otto. *Remember Me: Women and Their Friendship Quilts*. San Francisco, CA: The Quilt Digest Press, 1985.

—. *Pieced From Ellen's Quilt: Ellen Spaulding Reed's Letters and Story*. Dayton, Ohio: Halstead and Meadows Publishing, 1991.

Lohrenz, Mary Edna, and Anita Miller Stamper. *Mississippi Homespun: Nineteenth-Century Textiles and the Women Who Made Them*. Jackson, Mississippi: Mississippi Department of Archives and History, 1989.

Lucy A. Cannon Papers, MS. 198. Manuscripts Division, Maryland Historical Society Library.

M'Nally, Edward A. *The Importance of Education Particularly to Females...* Baltimore, MD, 1819.

MacDowell, Marsha, and Ruth D. Fitzgerald. *Michigan Quilts: 150 Years of a Textile Tradition*. East Lansing, MI: Michigan State University Museum, 1987.

MacNutty, W. Kirk. *Freemasonry: A Journey Through Ritual and Symbol*. New York: Thames and Hudson, Inc., 1991.

Macoy, Robert. *A Dictionary of Freemasonry*. New York: Bell Publishing Co., 1989.

Martin, Nancy J. *Pieces of the Past*. Bothell, WA: That Patchwork

Place, Inc., 1986.

—. *Threads of Time*. Bothell, WA: That Patchwork Place, Inc., 1990.

May Festival of Female Public School. Baltimore: James Lucas, 1850.

Melder, Keith E. *Beginnings of Sisterhood: The American Woman's Rights Movement, 1880 to 1850*. New York: Schocken Books, 1977.

Melder, Keith. "Mask of Oppression: The Female Seminary Movement in the United States." *New York History* 55 (July, 1974)

Meller, Susan, and Joost Elffers. *Textile Designs*. New York: Harry N. Abrams, Inc., 1991.

Monmonier, John F., M.D., J. F. C. Hadel and Edward J. Chaisty, M. D. *Report of the Board of Health*. Baltimore, MD: 1849.

Morey, Ann-Jenine. "Lamentation for the Minister's Wife, by Herself." *Women's Studies* 19 (1991).

Nelson, Cyril I., and Carter Houck. *Treasury of American Quilts*. New York: Greenwich House, 1982.

Nicoll, Jessica F. *Quilted for Friends: Delaware Valley Signature Quilts, 1840-1855*. Winterthur, DE: The Henry Francis duPont Winterthur Museum, 1986.

Ockenga, Starr. *On Women and Friendship: A Collection of Victorian Keepsakes and Traditions*. New York: Stewart, Tabori and Chang, 1993.

Oliver, Celia Y., ed. *55 Famous Quilts from the Shelburne Museum*. New York: Dover Publications, Inc., 1990.

Orlofsky, Patsy and Myron. *Quilts in America*. New York: McGraw-Hill Book Co., 1974.

Parry, Linda. *The Victoria and Albert Museum's Textile Collection: British Textiles from 1850 to 1900*. New York: Canopy Books, 1993.

Patapsco Female Institute, Reports of the Trustees, Visitor and Principal for 1844. Baltimore: John D. Troy, 1844.

Peck, Amelia. *American Quilts and Coverlets in The Metropolitan Museum of Art*. New York: Dutton Studio Books, 1990.

Pfeffer, Susanna. *Quilt Masterpieces*. New York: Park Lane, 1990.

Phelps, Mrs. *The Fireside Friend, or Female Student being Advice to Young Ladies on the Important Subject of Education*. Boston: Marsh, Capen, Lyon, and Webb, 1840.

Phillips, Barty. *Fabrics and Wallpapers: Sources, Design and Inspiration*. Boston: Little, Brown and Company, 1991.

Phoebe George Bradford, MS. 1077. Manuscripts Division, Maryland Historical Society Library.

Rae, Janet. *The Quilts of the British Isles*. New York: E. P. Dutton, 1987.

Ramsey, Bets, and Gail Andrews Trechsel. *Southern Quilts: A New View*. McLean, VA: EPM Publications, 1991.

Ramsey, Bets, and Merikay Waldvogel. *The Quilts of Tennessee: Images of Domestic Life Prior to 1930*. Nashville, TN: Rutledge Hill Press, 1986.

Randolph, M. *The Virginia Housewife*. Baltimore: Plaskitt and Cugle, 1831.

Regan, Jennifer. *American Quilts: A Sampler of Quilts and Their Stories*. New York: Gallery Books, 1989.

Ridgely, James L. *History of American Oddfellowship: The First Decade*. Baltimore: Published by James L. Ridgely, by Authority of the Grand Lodge of the United States I. O. O. F., 1878.

Roan, Nancy and Donald. *Lest I Shall Be Forgotten: Anecdotes and Traditions of Quilts*. Green Lane, PA: Goschenhoppen Historians, Inc., 1993.

Roan, Nancy, and Ellen J. Gehret. *Just a Quilt: A Folk Cultural Study and Source Book of Quilting Practices in and around the Goschenhoppen Region, 1840-1940*. Green Lane, PA: Goschenhoppen Historians Inc., 1984.

Roberson, Ruth Haislip, ed. *North Carolina Quilts*. Chapel Hill, N. C.: The University of North Carolina Press, 1988.

Rubin, Cynthia Elyce, ed. *Southern Folk Art*. Birmingham, AL: Oxmoor House, Inc., 1985.

Rumford, Beatrix T., and Carolyn J. Weekley. *Treasures of American Folk Art*. Williamsburg, VA: Colonial Williamsburg Foundation, 1989.

Safford, Carleton L., and Robert Bishop. *America's Quilts and Coverlets*. New York: E. P. Dutton and Co., Inc., 1972.

Sandweiss, Martha, Rick Stewart, and Ben W. Huseman. *Eyewitness to War: Prints and Daguerrotypes of the Mexican War, 1846-1848*. Fort Worth, TX: Amon Carter Museum, 1989.

Schiffer, Margaret B. *Historical Needlework of Pennsylvania*. New York: Bonanza Book, 1958.

Schoeser, Mary, and Celia Rufey. *English and American Textiles from 1790 to the Present*. New York: Thames and Hudson, 1989.

Schorsch, Anita. *Plain and Fancy: Country Quilts of the Pennsylvania-Germans*. New York: Sterling Publishing Co., Inc., 1992.

Semmes, Raphael. *Baltimore As Seen By Visitors, 1783-1860*. Baltimore, MD: Maryland Historical Society, 1953.

Shaw, Robert. *America's Traditional Crafts*. New York: Hugh Lauter Levin Associates, Inc., 1993.

Sienkiewicz, Elly. *Spoken Without a Word*. Washington, D. C.: The Turtle Hill Press, 1983.

—. *Baltimore Beauties and Beyond*. Vol. 1. Lafayette, CA C & T Publishing, 1989.

—. *Baltimore Album Quilts: Historic Notes and Antique Patterns*. Lafayette, CA: C & T Publishing, 1990.

—. *Baltimore Beauties and Beyond*. Vol. 2. Lafayette, CA: C & T Publishing, 1991.

—. *Design a Baltimore Album Quilt*. Lafayette, CA: C & T Publishing, 1992.

—. *Dimensional Appliqué: Baskets, Blooms, and Baltimore Borders*. Lafayette, CA: C & T Publishing, 1993.

—. *Baltimore Album Revival!* Lafayette, CA: C & T Publishing, 1994.

—. "The Fascinating Ladies: Ten Years of Baltimore Album Quilts." Lecture presented at the Maryland Historical Society's Lavish Legacies Symposium, Baltimore, June 17, 1994.

Sizer, Theodore and Nancy, Sally Schwager, et al. *To Ornament Their Minds*. Litchfield, CT: Litchfield Historical Society, 1993.

Sketches of Lives of Distinguished Females Written for Girls, 1833.

Smith, Linda Joan. "Moving in Secret Circles." *Country Home* 15, no. 5(October, 1993).

Specimens of Printing Types and Ornaments Cast at the Baltimore Types and Stereotype Foundry. Baltimore, MD: Lucas Brothers, 1854.

Susanna Warfield Diaries, MS. 760. Manuscripts Division, Maryland Historical Society Library.

Swan, Susan Burrows. *Plain and Fancy: American Women and their Needlework, 1700-1850*. New York: Holt, Rinehart, and Winston, 1977.

Swanson, Lynne, and Marsha MacDowell, ed. *Quilts from the Albert and Merry Silber Collection*. East Lansing, Michigan: Michigan State University Museum, 1988.

The Book of the Exhibition: Fifth Annual Exhibition of the Maryland Institute. Baltimore: from the Press of Sands and Mills, 1852.

The Book of the Exhibition: Fourth Annual Exhibition of the Maryland Institute. Baltimore: Printed by John Murphy & Co., 1851.

The Book of the Exhibition: Seventh Annual Exhibition of the Maryland Institute for the Promotion of the Mechanic Arts. Baltimore: from the Press of Sands & Mills, 1854.

The Book of the Exhibition: Sixth Annual Exhibition of the Maryland Institute for the Promotion of the Mechanic Arts. Baltimore: From the Press of Sands & Mills, 1853.

The Cold Water Almanac for 1843. Baltimore: William Barrett, 1843.

The Quilt Digest. Vol. 1-5. San Francisco, CA: The Quilt Digest Press, 1983-1987.

The Report of the Acts of Assembly Relating to Feme Coverts. The Commissioners Appointed to Codify the Laws of the State, Bel Air, MD: John Cox, 1858.

The Sun, May 23, 1843.

Third Annual Exhibition of the Maryland Institute for the Promotion of the Mechanic Arts, Held October 14th 1850, at Washington Hall, Baltimore. Baltimore: Printed by Sherwood & Co., 1850.

Tolles, Frederick B., Ph. D., ed. "Slavery and the Woman Question, Lucretia Mott's Diary of Her Visit to Great Britain to Attend the World's Anti-Slavery Convention of 1840." *Journal of the Friends' Historical Society*, supplement no. 23 (1952).

Twelker, Nancyann Johanson. *Women and Their Quilts: A Washington State Centennial Tribute*. Bothell, WA: That Patchwork Place Inc., 1988.

Uncoverings: Research Papers of the American Quilt Study Group. Vol. 1-14. San Francisco, CA: American Quilt Study Group, 1980-1993.

Vincent, Margaret. *The Ladies' Work Table: Domestic Needlework in Nineteenth-Century America*. Allentown, PA: Allentown Art Museum, 1988.

Weissman, Judith Reiter, and Wendy Lavitt. *Labors of Love: America's Textiles and Needlework, 1650-1930*. New York: Alfred A. Knopf, 1987.

Wellman, Judith. "The Seneca Falls Women's Rights Convention; A Study of Special Networks." *Journal of Women's History* 3, no. 1 (Spring, 1991).

Welter, Barbara. "The Cult of True Womanhood." *American Quarterly* 18 (Summer 1966): 151-174.

—. *Dimity Convictions, The American Woman in the Nineteenth Century*. Athens, Ohio: Ohio University Press, 1976.

Williams, Charlotte Allen. *Florida Quilts*. Gainesville, FL: University Press of Florida, 1992.

Williams, Judith. "The Seneca Falls Women's Rights Convention: A Study of Social Networks." *Journal of Women's History* 3, no. 1 (Spring 1991).

Wilson Papers. MS. 333.1. Manuscript Division, Maryland Historical Society Library.

Woodard, Thomas K., and Blanche Greenstein. *Classic Crib Quilts*. New York: Dover Publications, Inc., 1993.

Wynne, James, M. D. *Extract from the First Report of the Committee on Public Hygiene of the American Medical Association, Sanitary Report of Baltimore*. 1850.

Zegart, Terri. *Quilts, An American Heritage*. New York: Smithmark Publishers Inc., 1994.